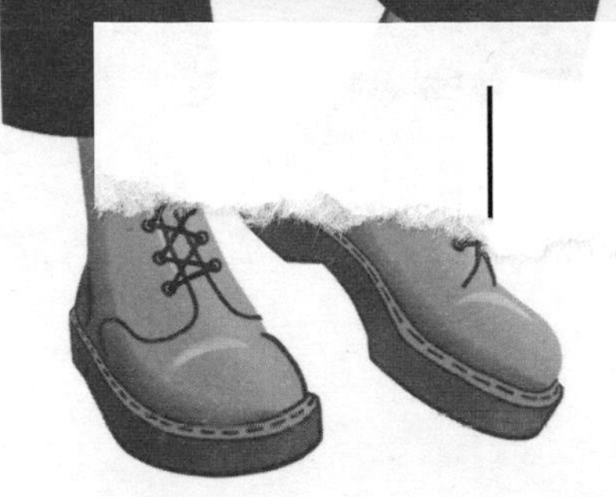

INSTRUCTIONS FOR A TEENAGE ARMAGEDDON

First published in Great Britain in 2021 by Wren & Rook

Hardback ISBN: 978 1 5263 6418 0
Export paperback ISBN: 978 1 5263 6431 9
E-book ISBN: 978 1 5263 6419 7
10 9 8 7 6 5 4 3 2 1

Wren & Rook
An imprint of Hachette Children's Group
Part of Hodder & Stoughton
Carmelite House
50 Victoria Embankment
London EC4Y 0DZ

An Hachette UK Company
www.hachette.co.uk
www.hachettechildrens.co.uk

Printed in UK

Additional images supplied by Shutterstock

INSTRUCTIONS FOR A TEENAGE ARMAGEDDON

30+ KICK-ASS WOMEN ON HOW TO TAKE OVER THE WORLD

WRITTEN AND CURATED BY **ROSIE DAY**

"Each time a woman stands up for herself, without knowing it possibly, without claiming it, she stands up for all women."

MAYA ANGELOU

DEDICATION

To all the girls as they grow, however that may be,

Hold on to your unique power, ever so tightly.

Rosie Day

CONTENTS

STAGING A TEENAGE ARMAGEDDON

I'm 14 years old and desperate to escape the humdrum town where I live. My head's vibrating on the window of the bus ride home and, as Taylor Swift blares out in my one working headphone, I'm wondering why no one mentioned that being a teenage girl was going to be *this hard*? Or, I don't know maybe they did, and I just wasn't listening? You see, I like *everything* and *nothing*.

My view of myself changes on a weekly – no – daily basis. But there is no guide book, no textbook and no answers to questions that I have (and would be too self-conscious to ask anyway!). I know I'm not alone in feeling this way and yet I feel it so deeply, but I manage to hide it with a forced smile that is just enough that no one notices.

These are meant to be the best years of my life, and yet I have to get up at 6am to spend countless hours studying subjects I hate, find a passion or hobby I excel in, all that while trying to maintain a type of social life that's worth posting about online. Or at least, this is what society is telling me I *should* be doing. I'm tired, and in my lowest moments I scroll through my contacts in my phone and realise I have no one to talk to about how I *really* feel. I find comfort in watching the traffic lights through the rainy bus

window: red, amber, green, there is something about their reliable nature and predictability that quells my anxiety. They remind me that things always change; the seasons, our feelings, our growing bodies. But change is for the better, and it's going to be OK.

And this book in your hands is to show you just that, but also to provide the support and reassurance that I wished I'd had then. I hope that as you dive into its pages, the words will embrace you like a giant, warm hug and won't let you go until you feel like you're armed to take on the world and feel empowered to tackle anything life throws at you.

And there are a whole host of topics to explore, written from personal and professional points of view we were able to source, including feminism, friendships, activism, skin care, being trans, mental health, consent, neurodiversity, self-love and many more.

There will be some topics that you may find triggering, tough or emotional, but I hope you agree that it's vital we don't shy away from these discussions; it's important that we have the language, understanding and tools to feel empowered enough to navigate them. That being said, please be kind to yourself, and if you need to take a break, skip a page or two, that's totally OK. At the end of the book, you can find a Resources section – a list of websites and organisations that I thought were particularly interesting, useful and important for all young people to know about, some of which can provide help and support to you on a number of issues we speak about within the book.

You might also spot the odd rude word (not many, I promise!) and mention of things that might not be age-appropriate for you right now, like sex or alcohol. Again, I wanted to keep these references in because in many cases our kick-ass contributors offer these as useful learning experiences to their younger selves.

I hope everyone can find something to relate to within these pages. This book is for every girl and young woman, everywhere.

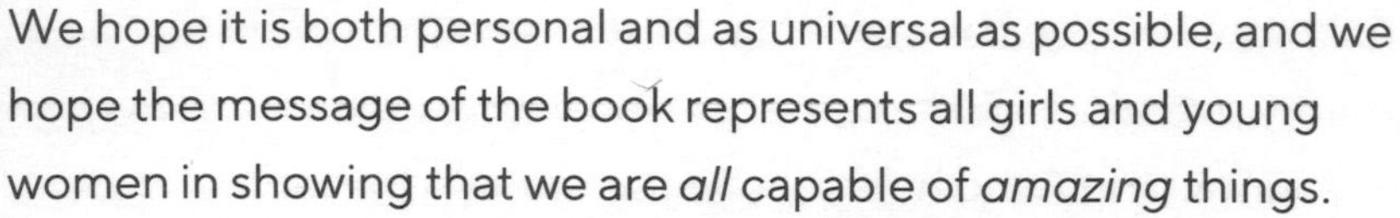

We hope it is both personal and as universal as possible, and we hope the message of the book represents all girls and young women in showing that we are *all* capable of *amazing* things.

I've also shared with you the stories of five of the most inspiring kick-ass women around today – women who I would definitely invite to join our Armageddon. And each chapter ends with a 10 top tips section, for you to take away some helpful snippets of advice. There's a lot coming at you as a young woman, and while your life might not be quite how you planned it right now (you might be sitting on your own rainy bus!), you have so much time, and I hope this book instills a sense of excitement for your future.

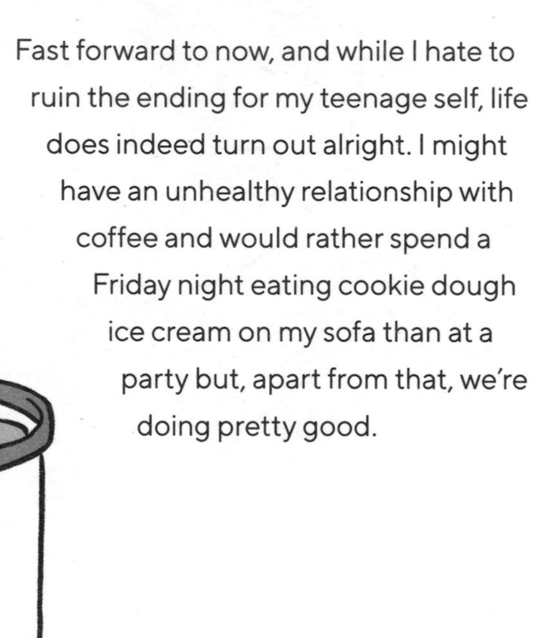

Fast forward to now, and while I hate to ruin the ending for my teenage self, life does indeed turn out alright. I might have an unhealthy relationship with coffee and would rather spend a Friday night eating cookie dough ice cream on my sofa than at a party but, apart from that, we're doing pretty good.

I wish there had been this guide back then, a helping hand to answer my questions. So here it is, a love letter to all you amazing, bright young things who have a power so strong you can

You just might not know it yet.

STEP 1
T
A

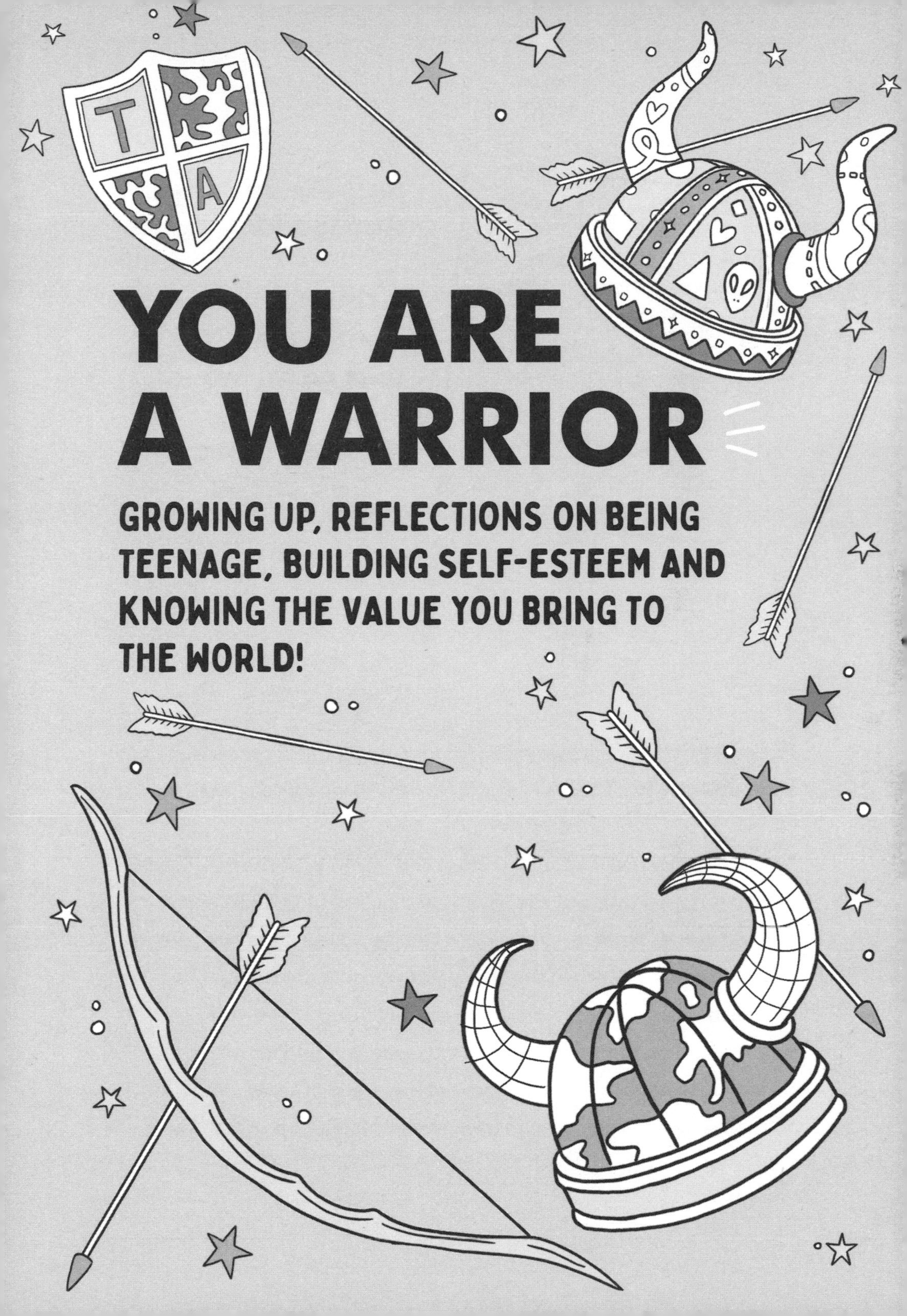

YOU ARE A WARRIOR

GROWING UP, REFLECTIONS ON BEING TEENAGE, BUILDING SELF-ESTEEM AND KNOWING THE VALUE YOU BRING TO THE WORLD!

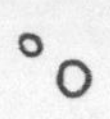

So we're starting an Armageddon, right?

A rebellion of young women ready to take on the world!

Agreed? Great.

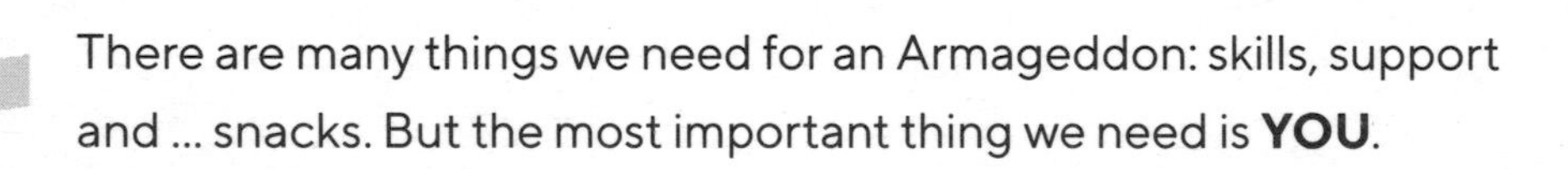

There are many things we need for an Armageddon: skills, support and ... snacks. But the most important thing we need is **YOU**.

So what *is* a warrior? I use to think it was some superhero/Viking hybrid ready to take out the villains with a few swift kicks and a cute costume. Then as I got older, I realised villains are not taken down by kicking them in the shins and warriors are not just in Marvel movies. No, warriors are everyday people, everyday *girls and women* walking down the street, rollerblading in the park, curled up watching the latest boxset – as normal as you and I. And no matter what is going on in their lives, they get up every day,

keep going and try to make the best of every situation. Sound familiar yet?

When I was a teenager, I was a patchwork quilt of all the successful women I looked up to. In fact, I was so busy trying to be them that I often didn't have time to embrace who *I* was. So don't be like me – be you! Because *teenage girls are warriors*. You are brave and bold. You have the potential to change things, to take over the world. And if you're not convinced by that, hopefully by the end of this book you will be ... Because here I've compiled notes, letters and essays from 32 awesome women who are going to help you on the road to staging a teenage Armageddon!

And before you say:

But I make mistakes and I beat myself up about them

or

I don't really like what I see in the mirror

or

To be honest, Rosie, my self-esteem could be better

BREATHE.

We'll cover all that.

Because contrary to popular belief (and cancel culture), we're allowed to make mistakes. When we're young, making mistakes is how we learn and grow as humans. I wouldn't know half the things

I know, if it wasn't for making some rather spectacular muck-ups. I like to think of them less as mistakes and more as Life Lessons, because it's how we *respond* to these mistakes that's important. We might not be able to control what happens in life, but we can control how we react.

And on that note, 'perfection'? It doesn't exist! And if you turn that longing and love you have for 'perfect', on to yourself, you'll find a power that no one can take away. In this book we want to equip you with the tools, armour and tactics to show that you are enough – exactly as you are. And if, these days, 'liking yourself' is a bit of a rebellious act, well, we're staging an Armageddon, we should do it as often as possible!

Right now, there is no one else on the planet quite like you – not a single soul on Earth.

On this floating space rock, there's only one of you. And considering the chances of being born are a minuscule 1 in 400 trillion (how amazing is that?), now we're here, we should enjoy it, as young warrior women with the ability to stage an Armageddon and even change the world.

Yes, you read that right, you're going to learn that, as young women, we can do WHATEVER we put our minds to. There is an incredible power in being a girl. And there is an incredible power in you.

And when us girls come together, the world better watch out. Because we are unstoppable ...

Bring on the Teenage Armageddon!

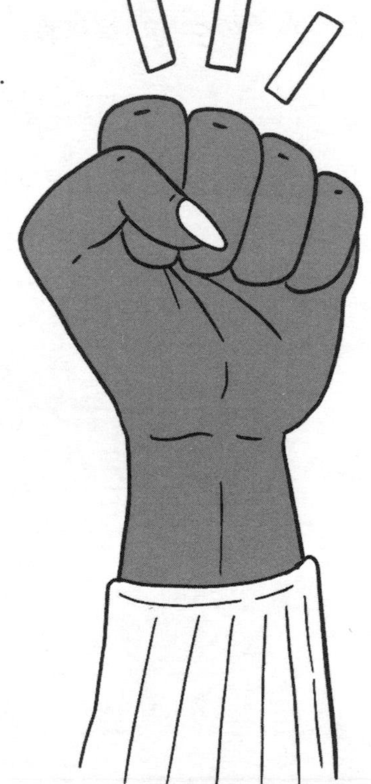

“I never, ever grew up as a young woman believing that my gender would stand in the way of anything I wanted to do.”

JACINDA ARDERN, PRIME MINISTER OF NEW ZEALAND.

A LETTER OF SELF-ACCEPTANCE TO 15-YEAR-OLD ME,
TANYA REYNOLDS, ACTOR

Dear Tanya

Ok. Put the hair dye down a sec, we just need to have a little talk.

It's FINE that you want to dye your hair black right now. It will look good. Or at least you'll look a bit more Emo, and it will counteract the fact that you don't really like Slipknot, you've never tried a cigarette, you don't like the taste of a single type of alcohol you've tried save Smirnoff Ice and that you're actually scared of everything. This bottle of hair dye will give your Myspace page that little edge you think it needs (it will also give you some brown patches because, hun, you need two bottles but whatever ...it's your first/only time and they'll mostly be at the back of your head). We just need to have a little chat about what is actually going on here. And oh, it's deeper than a My Chemical Romance song.

You want to dye your hair because you want to be someone else. That's fine. That's allowed. In fact it's a very normal part of being 15.

Generally it takes a lot of experimenting with your appearance to figure out WHO you actually are underneath it.

The issue here isn't with that, you could shave your head tomorrow if you wanted to (but dear God please do not, your complete lack of chin couldn't take it and you would look like a sperm). But here's the tea; you do not like yourself, at all, and you're trying to blend into the background life of the boy you are currently dating. You're diminishing everything that you are and everything that you like to be something that he and his friends – and basically any other people in the world apart from you – might approve of. You don't even realise you're doing it, and you won't, until you're

YAY OR NAY?

in your mid-20s in nother unfulfilling relationship and you realise that you have, yet again, made yourself a tiny piece of furniture in someone else's life.

You are so busy looking at how the people around you are doing things, that you are completely neglecting this weird and wonderful creature who stares back at you in the mirror before you smother her in eyeliner. Because she is shy, anxious and analytical, because she's scared to take an Ibuprofen, because her actual hobbies do not include skateboarding or 'going to gigs' but do include spending hours alone playing RollerCoaster Tycoon

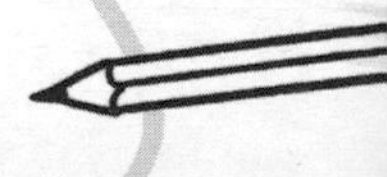

and reading romantic Vampire-centric fiction, you think she is worth significantly less than your cool, confident, facially pierced, hilarious, bass playing, mosh-pit-loving, don't-give-a-f**k counterparts.

You've ignored yourself for so long (and will unfortunately continue to do so for many years) that you don't actually understand yourself at all. You don't understand why everything makes you nervous. You don't understand why you can't walk into a room without assuming that everyone in that room hates you. You don't understand why you don't fancy your boyfriend. You sort of wish you weren't with your boyfriend, which you also don't understand because he's nice, isn't he? You don't understand why you're always sad for no reason.

And so you

shrink.

↓

o

I am sitting here, 28-year-old you, (and no, 28 is NOT as old as you think it is, so pick your jaw up right now, young lady), a tiny bit wiser, a tiny bit taller, a tiny bit less into My Chemical Romance, to throw down some truths. Because I have tried, over and over again ever since that bottle of black hair dye to be someone else, to try and fit someone else's idea of what anyone else wants. And it has taken me way into my twenties to actually stop and ask myself,

what do *I* want?

I spent so much energy worrying about how the world was receiving me, that I forgot to ask myself how I felt about anything at all. And so if given the magical opportunity to transcend time and get this letter to you, my 15-year-old self, I would love for you to know some things ...

I want you to know that you are FINE.

I want you to know that people whose identity is entirely centred around their taste in music can be a bit boring.

I want you to stop making yourself small. None of the boys you know are making themselves small.

I want you to know that being quiet is not a weakness.

I want you to know that all the things you hate about the way you look, will become your favourite things. Your 'freakishly long neck' is beautiful and one day it will become iconic in a yellow turtleneck.

I want you to know that: **YOU DON'T HAVE TO DATE A BOY JUST BECAUSE HE WANTS TO DATE YOU!**

I want you to stop undermining the things you feel.

I want you to know that bi-sexuality and sexual fluidity are legit, as are those feelings you just love to smother down, so for the love of GOD, press pause on these boys whose personalities are 'plays drums' and go and kiss a girl, for goodness sake.

I want you to pay attention in all your classes, because, yes, we know you want to be an actress so you feel like you 'Don't need to know geography or physics' but hun, you do. You will be an actress, but if you don't pay attention to other stuff outside of drama, you will be a very boring person.

I want you to know that it is actually very cool that you just want to sit in your room alone, writing fiction at the weekends.

I want you to know that you don't have to fit into a box. Boxes are boring. I want you to be kind to yourself and to your body. Because you're going to be with her forever, through everything. Make her a nice place to live.

So, there it is my sweet little llama. Dye your hair whatever colour you want, but in exchange for a whole year of photographs that I have to look back on of you (looking like a ghoul whose hair doesn't match her eyebrows) do me a favour and listen to yourself. Now go forth. RollerCoaster Tycoon isn't going to play itself.

Love Tanya xx

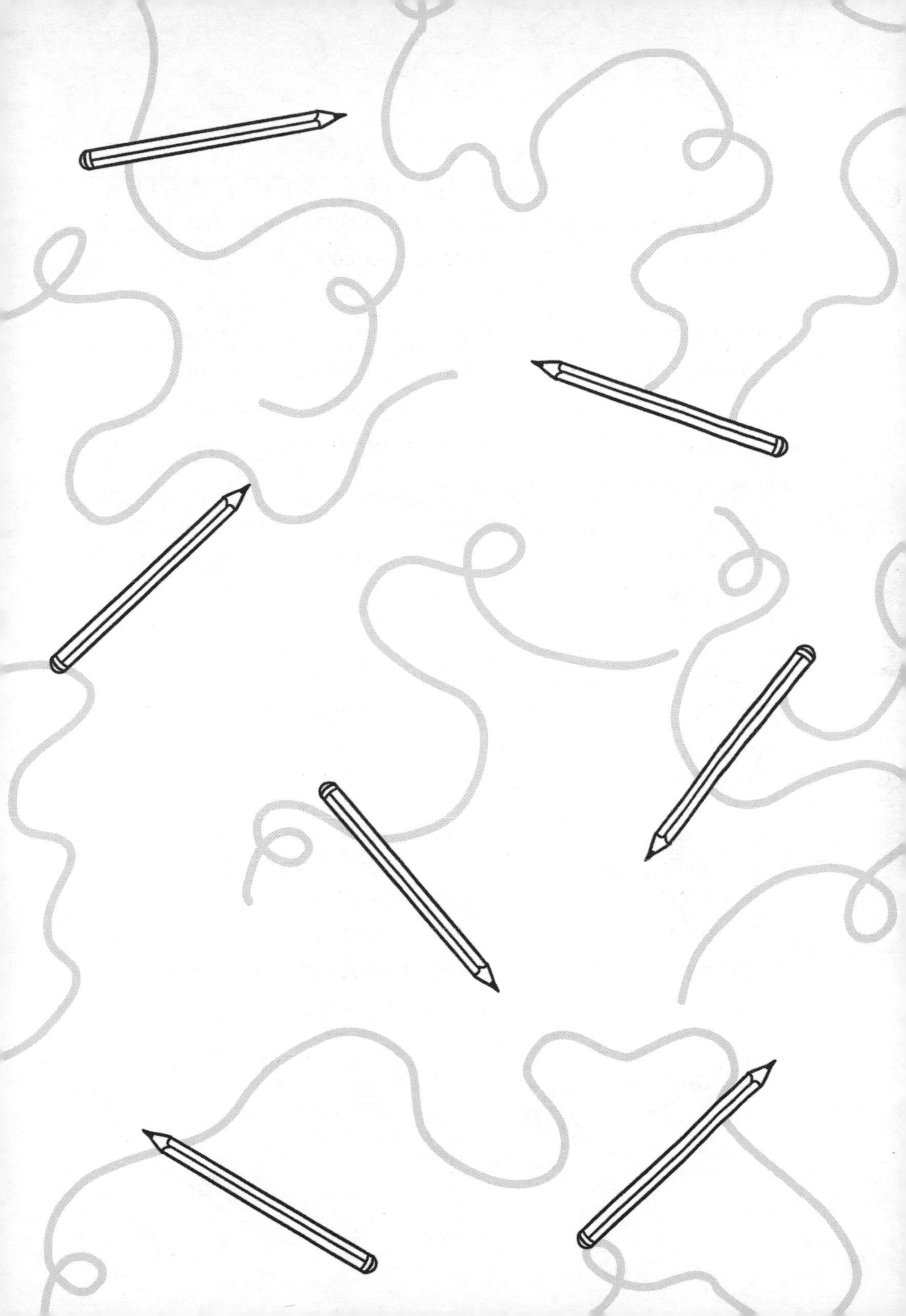

~~**FAIL TO PREPARE**~~ **PREPARE TO FAIL,** GEMMA STYLES, PODCASTER AND WRITER

When I was fifteen I would've wanted to open this book and have someone tell me EXACTLY how to avoid all the mistakes that other people make.

Instructions to skip the awkward phase, please! Everyone else can do it the messy way (i.e, those people who haven't been careful enough to read the book).

As teenagers we probably all have a vague vision of ourselves in our mid-20s; where we might work, what city we want to live in, what our friends will be like. That's about as far ahead as my imagination went as a teen – 25 seemed like the pinnacle of adulthood.

The mid-20s version of me was a teacher. She knew exactly what she was doing, she was content and confident; secure in the knowledge that she'd followed The Plan and it had all paid off.

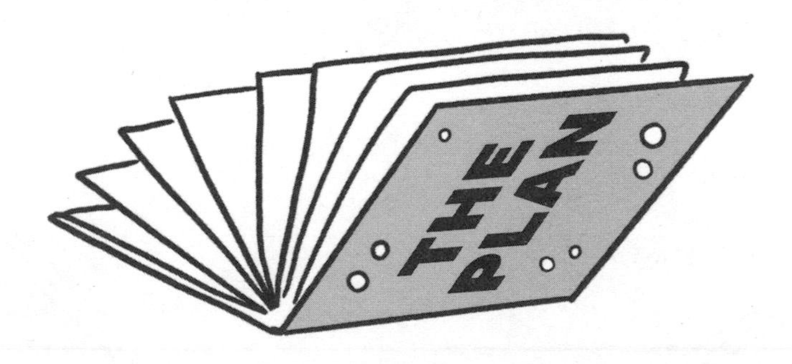

I thought that it should go something like this:

- [x] GCSEs
- [x] A-levels
- [x] Degree
- [x] Secure job in degree field

That's absolutely not what happened. Actually for me it went something like this:

- [x] GCSEs
- [x] A-levels
- [x] University
- [x] Major depression
- [x] Leave of absence
- [x] Unemployment
- [x] Officially 'drop out'
- [x] Childminding
- [x] New university

- [x] *Degree*
- [x] *Exhaustion*
- [x] *Job in adjacent field*
- [x] *Freelancing on the side*
- [x] *Self-employment*

That timeline does end nicely in my mid-20s though, which works well for this story.

So let's dive into that middle section, where it gets sticky ...

I had passed my first year of university, I loved my friends, I loved the city and where I lived. The Plan seemed to be doing its job! But where I 'should' have been happy, I wasn't. Something started to feel like a mistake. As new course modules started and classes changed, I wasn't seeing a life I wanted at the end of the path anymore. I don't know if it's possible to fully untangle that situation from the depression I suffered, but I ended up at home for Christmas break in my second year and would wake up every morning and cry. It was truly an awful time. I couldn't make myself

revise for January exams. I would go back, fail them, and then what? Eventually, not knowing what to do, my mum called my old head of sixth form who came over for a chat. Through my tears I admitted, like it was the worst thing in the world, how badly I didn't want to do my course anymore, and she said, 'So don't.'

FREEDOM.

Someone suddenly gave me

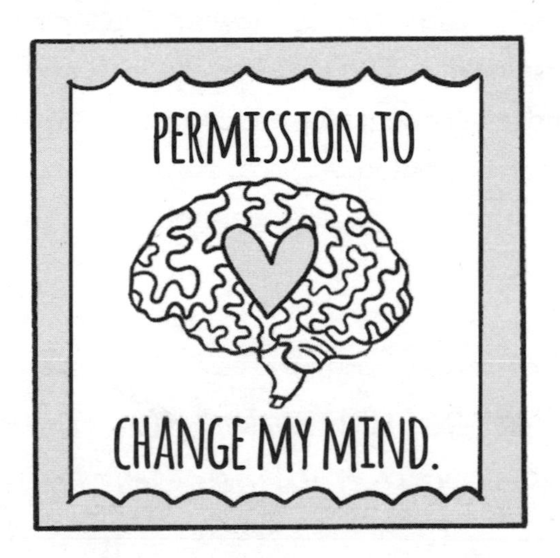

I don't know why I didn't feel like I had that before. Maybe it's just different when it comes from someone impartial. Anyway, I was well on the path to becoming a drop-out and that failure was infinitely more comfortable than continuing to try and succeed in something I didn't want.

I changed my plan, and then I changed it again. And again. (The rest of the timeline.) Honestly, to say I have a 'plan' even now would be ... a very loose use of the word. There were lots of painful personal experiences in there that nobody would choose for themselves. But without those parts, I wouldn't be who I am right now, and I wouldn't have the experience that will continue to be valuable to me.

Through our failures we develop empathy and compassion. The huge success of failure-based books and podcasts such as Elizabeth Day's legendary *How to Fail* exemplifies what an appetite there is for learning about how other people feel they've failed. Since starting my *Good Influence* podcast and asking listeners to send in questions, I've noticed how often people want to ask someone the question

What advice would you give to your younger self?

Often this question does come from young people, but not always.

Even if you're no longer a teen, I think the root of it comes from wanting to know how others have achieved their success, or how to emulate someone you admire, without making the mistakes that they made. We want to know the smooth, painless path with no bumps and nothing to trip us up. We want to know everything right away and to bypass the awkward phase of testing and trying and getting things wrong. Why reinvent the wheel? If our role models would just share their secrets then surely things could fall into place for us so much more easily?

The fact of it is, we don't get to skip making our own mistakes, so reframing how you think about them right from the outset is a good way to seize some control. The older you get the more you realise that sharing stories of our failures isn't about gawking at others' inadequacies or even really commiserating with them.

No, failing, or at the very least, feeling like you've failed, is a universal human experience, but one that we're usually not brought up to prepare for.

Especially as a teenager, people around you tell you that you should shoot for the stars, that you can do anything and *be* anything that you want to be. And they *should* tell you that, because you should aim that high. You are a swirling mass of potential wrapped up with a bow. You're a damn gift! And there's so much time! No one should go around telling teenagers not to aim for too much in case they don't get it – that is certainly not what I'm saying – but this narrative does have the potential to leave us feeling completely blind-sided when things don't work out the way we had hoped; when we fail.

So, knowing that you have to set off down a path that will likely lead you past some unfortunate setbacks, dodgy decision-making and a touch of heartbreak ... What advice could I possibly give you?

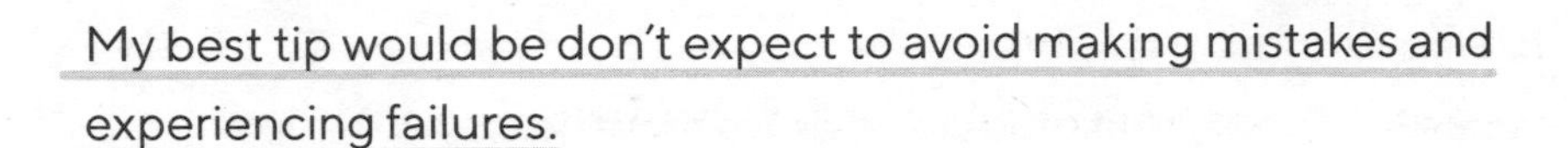

My best tip would be don't expect to avoid making mistakes and experiencing failures.

Don't wait for a magical day when you wake up and feel like a grown up and everything seems simpler – it doesn't come.

You might have more responsibility and you might feel like you know yourself better, but the older I get and the more people I talk to about this I realise it just doesn't happen in the way we expect as teenagers. I still wonder if being a parent is the thing that makes you feel like you know what you're doing all of sudden, but according to the mums I know, that's not the case either.

Listen to other people when they talk about their failures. Not to try and avoid them but to try and accept that you, like them, are a

flawed and imperfect human being. And like them, you can still be successful and a role model and achieve wonderful things.

If you're waiting to reach an imaginary milestone before you make a change, or start a project, or stop doing something that makes you unhappy... DON'T. Being a couple of years older isn't guaranteed to bring the wisdom or the freedom from failure that you might expect. And not to be all *We're Going on a Bear Hunt* (I hope people still know that book.) but, 'We've just got to go through it'. So start now.

You can do hard things. You can do things that scare you. You can say no, at any time, for any reason. Nobody has it all figured out. Ask for help.

Fail and try again.

Fail and choose something else.

Look forward to your life. Because

everything

will be

okay.

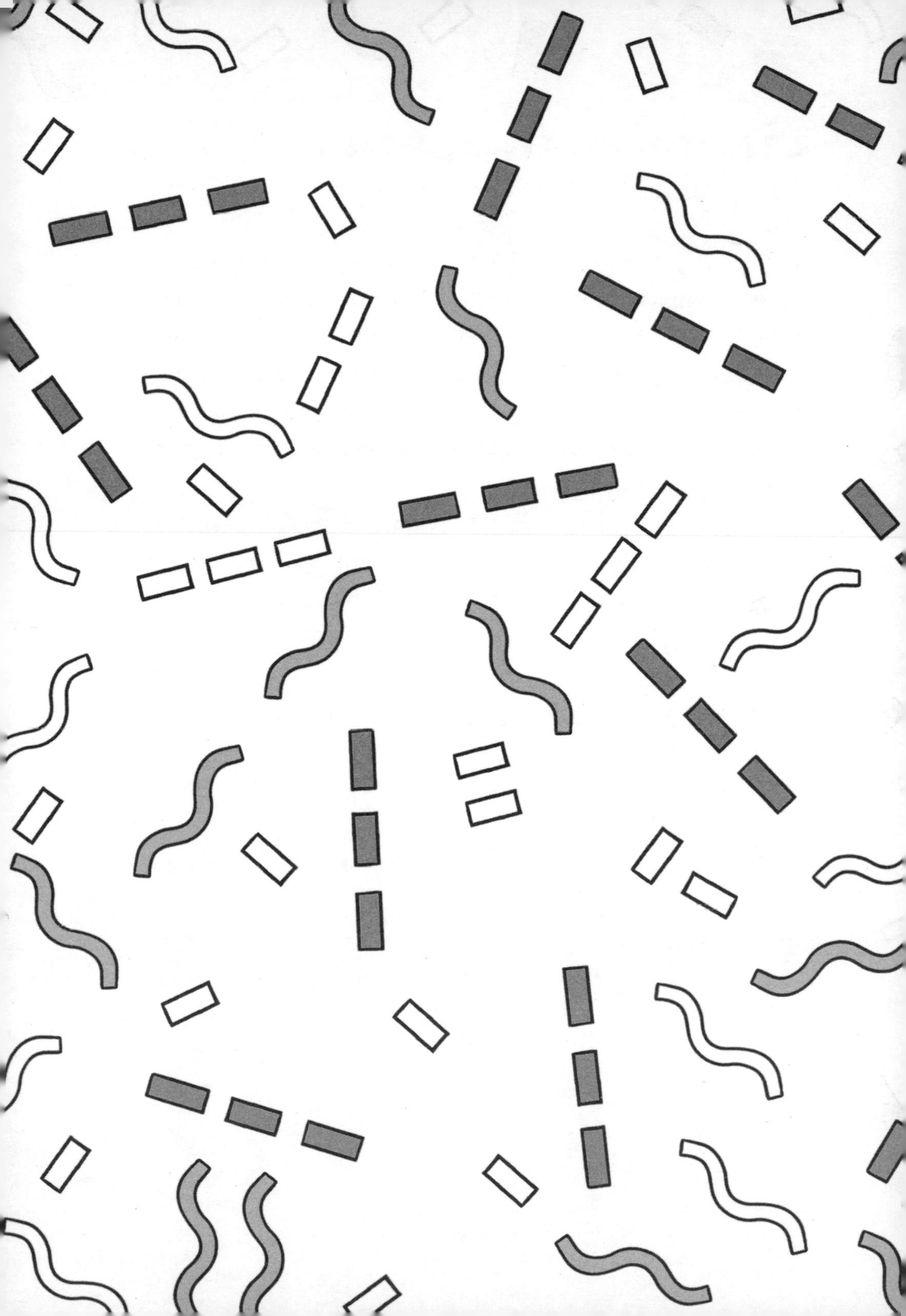

A LETTER TO TEENAGE ME,
NELL HUDSON, ACTOR

Dear Teenage Nell,

Hi! It's me – you! I think about you a lot. I talk to you in my head sometimes when something happens that I know you would appreciate. Things like cool jobs I've booked, that time The Trunchbull from the movie *Matilda* stuck her fingers in my mouth on the set of *Call The Midwife*, the kindness I now demand from boys, (well, men) that I'm sorry you didn't always get.

I know it's too late now – and if you're still as stubborn and wilful as I remember you being – you aren't going to take anyone's advice anyway, but here's 10 things I would tell you if there was even a tiny chance of you listening:

1. Start using a gradual tanning moisturiser. Bin that spray-on orange stuff you've been using.
2. Find a medium-brown eyebrow pencil and start using it.
3. Try yoga. Keep at it. You'll like it, and it'll make you feel better in both body and mind.

4 Do your homework on time. Just do it. You're so stressed all the time, in a constant state of anxiety because you need to come up with yet another excuse to give to your teachers about why it's not done. Just bloody do it. Do it the second you get home, with a nice snack and a glass of juice. You'll be finished by the time *The Simpsons* starts at 6.

5 Dump him. Dump him. Dump him. I know, I know – you love him. But he's going to break your heart again and again, so just break it yourself now and save yourself years of agony and intense damage to your self-esteem.

6 Doing people favours and paying for things doesn't make them like you. It makes them use you. I know you think you're just a natural 'giver', but test-drive not being so generous all the time and see what happens. I think people will respect you more. Instead, ask people questions about themselves – about their families and siblings, about what books they're reading or TV shows they're watching. Ask them anything. And try and be real with them back. Being vulnerable around others lets them see the real you and is very bonding.

7 Therapy might be a good idea for you, my love. Ask mum and dad if you can have some; discuss the options of CBT (cognitive behavioural therapy) versus counselling. I know you think you have to be a certain way to make people like you, and I know you're hurting, but talking to someone helps – I promise.

8 I hate to break it you, but you're a nerd. You love learning, you love reading, and I'm so proud of how good you are at maths. So stop wasting time pretending to be less intelligent

than you really are, stop chasing the 'popular' kids, and go and hang out with the other nerds. You'll be so much happier. (And here's a secret: when you grow up, those nerds are way cooler than the popular kids.)

9. Let go. I know it's hard, but being self-conscious and trying to look cool is the biggest con in the world. You're so goofy and silly and funny in secret. These days, I let that side of me out all the time, I'm not embarrassed by it, and it's something I love about myself and I believe attracts the right people to me. People who are goofy and silly, too. People who are kind and don't take themselves too seriously, who apologise freely, who are thoughtful, and sensitive, and love you.

10. I love you.

Nell (nearly 30 years old) (yep, I'm old.) xxx

ALEXANDRIA OCASIO-CORTEZ
THE NOTORIOUS AOC
'We have to have the courage to say, we can do better'

When it comes to politics, there is no doubt that now, more than ever, we need more women front and centre showing up and running the world. On a global scale, men are largely responsible for deciding how societies are run – and that includes voting on women's issues. But thankfully it looks like times are (slowly) a-changing. In 2020 we saw super-queen Kamala Harris become the first-ever Madam Vice President and over in New York there is a fierce and amazing young Democrat taking on the world and winning …

At the age of 29, Alexandria Ocasio-Cortez (also known as AOC) became the youngest woman ever to be elected to the United States Congress. She also achieved this by beating 10-term undefeated Democrat Joe Crowley.

Growing up in the Bronx, an underprivileged area of New York City she believed her postcode was her destiny. AOC was a highly intelligent young woman with a passion for science, but it was the death of her father that was the catalyst for her switch into politics. After witnessing first-hand the hardship of not being able to afford medical insurance or basic social care, Alexandria made it her mission to change things for ordinary working people.

She quit her Biochemistry major and switched to Economics and International Relations whilst working 18-hour shifts to support herself and her family. Many times she has said she never intended to become a politician, but her deep-rooted desire to help people and fight the injustices of the world became the drive for her to succeed.

Her main focus as a politician is to bring social injustices and issues to the attention of Congress. AOC has said multiple times she doesn't want to become President of the USA, which is a shame because I can't help but think she would rock it ...

GIRLS & AUTISM, PAIGE LAYLE, INFLUENCER & NEURODIVERSITY ACTIVIST

I'm sure most children believe they are different, but for me, I knew I was ...

How did I know? Well, as a young girl I was stressed all of the time, in ways that affected my ability to function on an day-to-day basis. I would cry a lot from sheer overwhelm, while at the same time was laser-focused on planning

Every.
Single.
Aspect of my life.

Nothing could go off the plan – like, EVER. Yep, I was a perfectionist. Things just *had* to be a certain way, or my world would crumble. No one put this pressure on me though, my non-typical brain just decided things needed to be a certain way, or it wasn't okay.

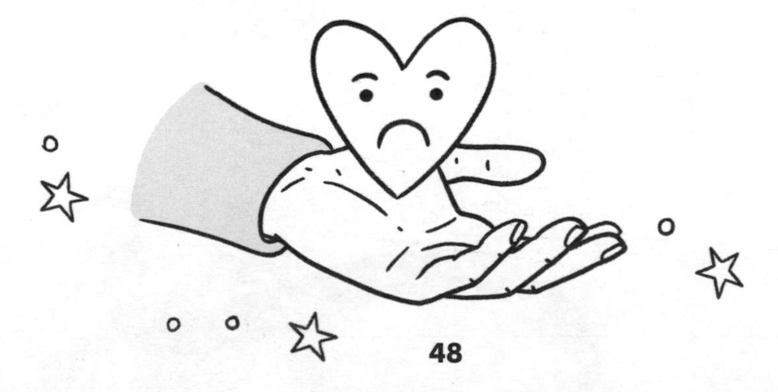

I was frustrated that even my clothes felt strange on my body, I never understood people, nor had many friends – and I always seemed to be the last one to get a joke. Oh and I could never decipher the meaning of words in English class. I was just so different, and no one understood. It sometimes felt like no one could help me.

I attempted to end my life when I was 14. Luckily, I can speak on this today because it was unsuccessful. But it wasn't until I ended up in the hospital that doctors were shocked that I had not already been assessed considering how I'd felt my entire life. I was diagnosed with a plethora of disorders, with one common denominator.

I'm autistic.

Autism is a neurodiverse condition, meaning that my brain is wired differently from most other people's.

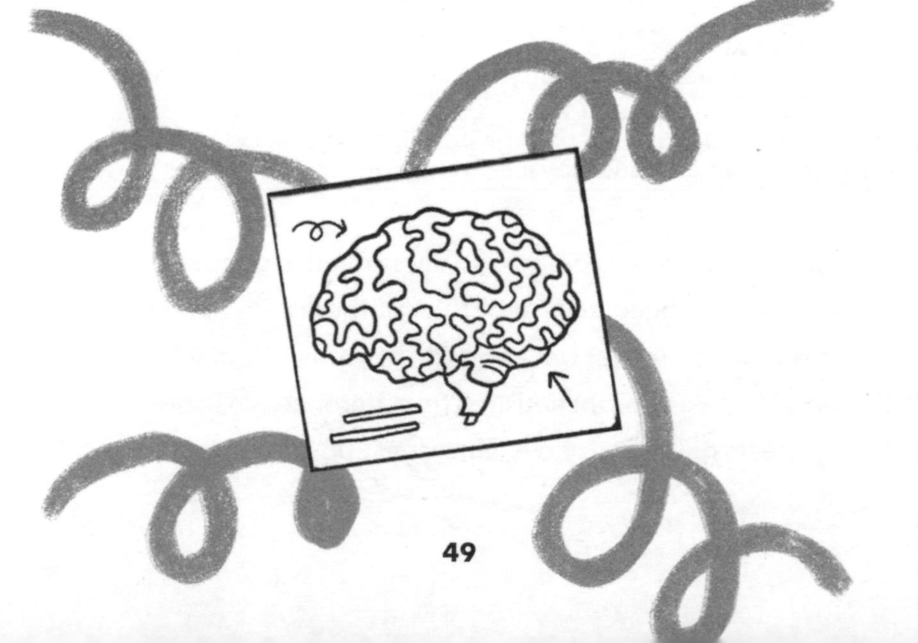

Things like society's rules and norms, social hierarchy and things like facial and body expressions don't register in my brain.I rely on facts, planning and doing things a certain way. I also have a lot of sensory issues with things like touch, light and interoception, specifically. Interoception is the ability to identify internal sensations like hunger, thirst, being too hot or cold.

Oh and I really do like to be on my own to recharge.

My claim to fame (as you might call it) was when I started speaking out online about autism and how it can affect people – but particularly highlighting the differences in how autism is represented in girls and boys.

It's true that autism was only originally studied in people who were AMAB (assigned male at birth), but there aren't that many neurological differences between AMAB autism, and AFAB (assigned female at birth) autism. The differences lie in how society treats girls versus boys. Girls are supposed to be sensitive.

Girls are supposed to overreact, and cry, show discomfort, and be organized. We learn these traits growing up – and society comes to expect them from us. When a boy is stressed, anxious and sensitive, it's seen as 'abnormal'. *Obviously there must be a problem?* As a consequence, boys are typically diagnosed much sooner than girls.

When I was 15, most of my female autistic friends were in their 20s and 30s, and most of my male autistic friends were diagnosed before the age of 6.

Go figure.

Of course, we all have the same underlying struggles with autism. We all have sensory issues. We all have meltdowns. We all have trouble coping with change. We all are confused with how society runs and underlying meanings to tone and phrases. But the biggest difference is some of us weren't taken seriously. A lot of AFABs are excellent 'maskers'– that's where you hide your autistic traits and copy others around you to try to seem more 'normal'.

Imagine it like this: you're an alien trying to learn how to be a human, but if anyone finds out you're an alien, they'll kill you, so you have to try really, really hard to appear as human as possible. AFABs are more likely to be better at masking because of the pressures society puts on women to behave in a certain way.

Masking is incredibly exhausting, but it's often what autistic girls have to do. Now that I'm older and understand myself better, I am trying to take the mask off and live as my authentic self. I'm now 20 years old, and I am still trying to get it right.

So my mission now is to show autistic people all over the world that we deserve to be loved and accepted for WHO we are.

I advocate that rather than asking neurodiverse people to change, society needs to find a way to include us. Our non-neurotypical brains are inspired, creative and amazing. Our talents deserve to be showcased and not assimilated to a version of 'normal'.

Normal doesn't exist so why should I hide who I really am?

I want to say to you from the bottom of my heart that if you suspect there's something different about you, don't be afraid of searching for a diagnosis. I know, a formal diagnosis can seem super scary, but to me, it saved my life and changed it for the better.

It's so empowering to have that connection with your brain and to finally be able to understand it and yourself. And it is SO empowering to understand your own needs, set your own boundaries, and be in a position to better yourself.

If we all unite on this, we can build a better world – one where everyone's differences can be embraced and where we can ALL thrive, live authentically and be happy.

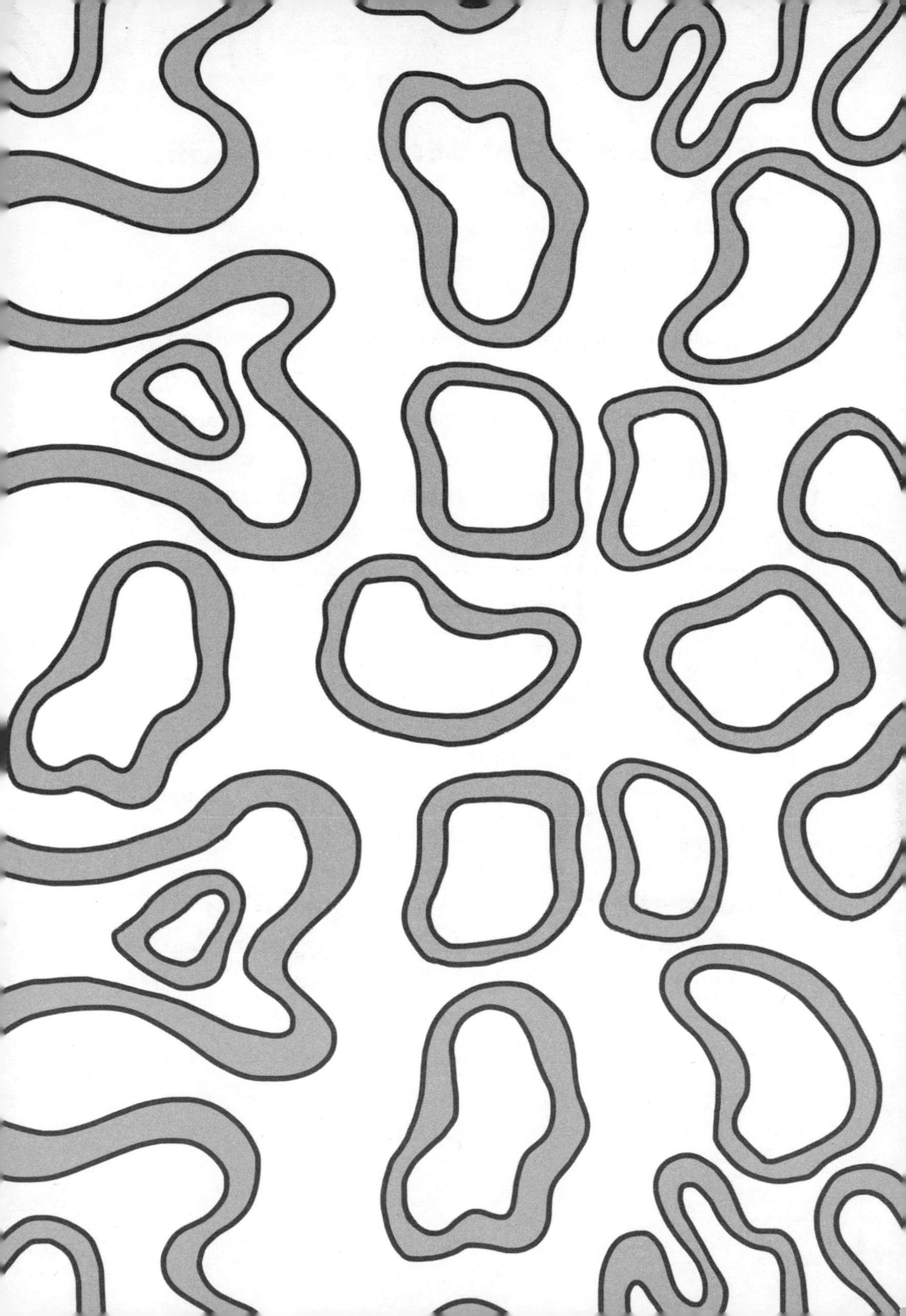

REFLECTIONS ON BEING TEENAGE, ALEXA DAVIES, ACTOR

I tried to think of a clever simile to describe being a teenage girl, but the closest I got was this:

'Being a teenage girl is like trying to complete a boot camp assault course because you think your body's not quite right, whilst having to yell out answers to academic and personal questions throughout. Also – SURPRISE! – you're having quite a heavy period and everyone you know is filming it on their phones to put it on social media'. It's exhausting.

I hate the word 'teenage'. I mean that in many senses. I did not enjoy a huge portion of my teenage years at all, and wouldn't do it again if you paid me. (Actually, that is a massive lie. I have a price for everything, and I would definitely do it all again if I could get a massive house with a walk-in fridge out of it.) More importantly, I am not a fan of the word because it's used to describe a period of time that massively influences our lives. I would like to change the word 'teenage', because I don't believe the title really fits the job description.

'Teenage girl' literally means a 'female, between the ages of 13 and 19', but some of the inconveniences and burdens can start years before that, right? That's when your brain and body start to change. Puberty can start in some girls at the incredibly young age of 7. So let's scrap the term 'teenage girl' and pick something else? (Don't get me wrong though, I have no idea what we would change it to! I typed in

names for strong women

and thought I had a few solid options but it turns out most of them were, historically, used as insults ... sigh.)

But let's look on the positive side. If you're reading this as a 14 year old then you shouldn't worry because, as you'll have figured by now, puberty and adolescence happens over the course of 10 years, and you barely notice it happening most days. When you are in the thick of it all, it feels like it's all happening gradually. There'll be times where you really have to sit down, check in with yourself and be reminded that there is nothing *wrong* with you, you're just going through a process of change. And that's incredible, when you think about it.

Everything else pales in comparison. Babies take 9 months to grow in the womb. Caterpillars transform into butterflies in less than 3 weeks. Christ! Julius Caesar was only head of the Roman Empire for 2 years. You're in it for the long haul. Remember that.

Relish in it.

Take your time.

Take.
Your sweet.
Time.

Because you can. Because you have it. If I could go back and tell myself anything, it would be to take your time. There is no rush at all. Read books. Watch films. Go outside. Listen to other people's stories. Learn from them. Being an adult is great, but there's no prize for winning the race to get here. Take your time.

You may feel like you need to be on top of things. You don't. Being on top of things is really hard. Even tiny things, like knowing when your period is coming or applying flawless eyeliner. As I write this, I'm in my mid-20s and I personally pride myself on having my

shit impressively together for a woman my age, but my God, that doesn't mean I'm on top of everything. I have no idea what I'm doing. I'm still learning. I'm taking my time.

Maybe we should start a summer camp for girls who are turning 13 and give them a course on what's about to happen. Maybe I'll run it. We'll take 6 weeks near a beautiful lake, to sit by a campfire and discuss all of our dreams, fears and worries. We'll go on 'No Question is a Stupid Question' hikes, where I personally would throw out there:

"Why do magazines want me to stop eating delicious bread?"

On departure day, you'd be handed a gift bag, the contents of which would include a personalised, reusable water bottle*, a USB pre-loaded with info on feminine hygiene products, contraceptive advice, a small bag of your favourite biscuits and this book. Obviously the bag itself would be a sustainably made tote that you will have hand-embroidered in the sewing workshop, entitled 'If your clothes don't fit, here's how to make them. It's not that your body is the wrong shape, the clothes are.' Admittedly the workshop titles might need some work. We'd have a bloody good time though, I'll tell you that for nothing. (A price for everything, see.) It would be a summer to say goodbye to over a decade of being a child, and hello to many decades of being an adult. Akin to many popular coming-of-age films like *Booksmart, Eighth Grade & Midsommar***.

* Stay hydrated guys, it's the fountain of youth.

** Kidding! At least, I think am. I don't know. I haven't seen it.

COMING OUT & PROUD,
BEL PRIESTLEY, LGBTQ+ INFLUENCER

Hi, I'm Bel and I'm a proud transgender woman.
It took me a while to get to this place where I could say those words, but at the age of 17 (as I write) with my whole life ahead of me, I can finally say I am proud of who I am. I'm a young trans girl growing up online and although I love being a 'influencer' it comes with a lot of negatives. However, I've learnt to look past the negativity because I love me for ME! But don't get me wrong, I wasn't always this way ...

OK, let's take it back to the beginning.

I grew up in a small town in England where I never felt like I fitted in. No matter what I did or who I pretended to be, nothing ever felt right. It was like I had this constant urge to change, whether that was a new hobby, new friends or new style ... but nothing ever filled this hole. It was like I was an incomplete puzzle waiting for that final piece.

I'd always dreamt of being a woman. Nothing sounded better to me than the thought of having long, flowing hair, running round the playground in a summer dress, playing with the other girls at school. And being a curious little boy, all I could do was wonder about what it would be like to be a girl because of the constant pressure of everyone around me to 'be a boy'. That meant playing football with the boys where I'd be the last one picked, shoved in goal and have everyone booting a ball at me for 45 minutes straight. I know fun, right?

By the age of 11, after watching *Twilight* and having the biggest crush on Jacob, I concluded that I fancied men and, after a good while of sneaking to the living room to kiss the *Twilight* DVD cover, I decided it was time to tell someone. So, I told a few friends, who told a few friends, who ended up telling *everyone*. Thinking it would be a massive shock to everyone's systems, I later found out that everyone had known for years (I'd kept it on the down-low unbelievably well, clearly). But to be honest it wasn't that bad.

One night, just after my 12th birthday, I made one of the best decisions of my life – and that led me to where I am today. I made the awful decision to try fake tan on my face. Now, if you have ever tried fake tan, you'll know it doesn't always go to plan. So, after my late-night tanning adventure, I woke up with a wonky, bright orange square on my face (because who tans their whole face anyway? – said no one). After scrubbing 19 layers off my skin, I came to the conclusion that this mess was not coming off, so I ran to mum, she grabbed her makeup bag and slathered me with concealer ready for school. Even though it was only a tiny bit of concealer I felt invincible. Eventually this turned into a daily thing and the tiny bit of concealer turned it to a bright blue smoky eye and red lip for a casual trip to the supermarket. An yet, something still didn't feel right.

Then, late one night I was on YouTube, streaming my daily dose of beauty tutorials when a video popped up in my recommendations with the title

It featured a stunning woman as the thumbnail and my curious little ass clicked the video. I had never seen a transgender person

before – I didn't even know the concept existed! The closest I'd ever been to a trans person was my uncle Bill wearing a party wig for Halloween and calling himself Stacey, with a pint of beer in his hand. My brain could not compute that this was a real thing. I clicked on the video and within two minutes I was balling my eyes out! It finally all made sense. That was it! The missing puzzle piece had been found. I had no doubt from that point on that I was a woman, but now I was set with the dreaded task of Coming Out.

I knew my parents would accept me as they already knew I was gay and feminine, so telling them felt like a big relief. Telling my close friends was also a comfort as I knew now we were all on the same page. Looking back I don't think any of us had any clue about how my life would change.

Coming out is a scary thing and from someone who has been there, done that and got the T-shirt, I can honestly tell you that the relief you will feel afterwards makes it all worth it.

When coming out to your family or friends, my first bit of advice would be to see how they talk about others from the LGBTQ+ community and if they are accepting of them.

Before I came out as trans to my parents, I asked that we all sit down to watch a transgender documentary to see how they would react, and because my dad ended up crying (he found it emotional) I took that as a pretty good sign that it was going to be okay. Remember your emotional, mental (and physical) safety is number one priority.Sit them down when you think is the right time and tell them how you've been feeling. Hopefully, even if not straight away, eventually they will come round and get on board with it.

That said, after coming out as Bel, I had the toughest few years of my life and having my parents by my side got me through it. At school, it was pretty much considered acceptable to treat me badly or disrespect me because I was trans, and as much as my peers didn't agree with the bullying, they didn't want to be outcasts for defending me either – so I was pretty much on my own. Everyone wants to fit in and because being trans wasn't exactly the 'cool' thing to do, I ended up hating myself for something I couldn't change. I hated being who I was because I just wanted to be normal. But what I've realised now is that it's our differences that make us who we are and what makes us unique.

Trans is not a burden. Trans is beautiful – and the quicker you realise that no matter who you are, what you do or where you come from, you deserve the world. Do not let people treat you less than you're worth. Growing up a trans teen taught me that no matter what you do in this world there will always be someone who doesn't agree with you, so what is the point of being or doing something that you don't believe in? And when something happens to bring you down or make you want to quit, just think of it as another barrier to break through, another person to prove wrong or another reason to keep striving to be great.

Back then, I was my own worst enemy and I would believe the negatives that people would throw at me because I thought it was what I deserved. Whereas now I *know* that I'm a good person and I'm proud of who I've become, so if anyone tries to tear me down,

I don't even blink an eye. I know that I've come so far. And so can you!

If I could go back and tell that little boy the things I've achieved at the age of 17 he would be flabbergasted. (Did you expect me to feature in a book and not say a cool word once?) No way would little me have expected to have the platform or the career I now have in front of me. So why would it be any different for you? You're here to achieve greatness and you will!

So, this was just a gentle reminder to say

and I honestly can't wait to see what you become.

SKY DIVING, STEPPING STONES, FAILURE & ME, MAXINE HERON, TRANS MODEL & ACTIVIST

Imposter syndrome is very real, and it relishes in my failures. It thrives on my shortcomings, binges on my mistakes. I'm used to the feeling of occupying a mediocre middle ground – an awkward space – not quite breaking the surface into any realm of importance, but seemingly drifting by, just enough to meet the standard. Existing in the interim feels like purgatory. At least, it constantly feels as though I'm living in an interim; so visible in my mediocrity, and yet so invisible in my successes.

See, failure is just that; a feeling that you haven't quite won.

But if failures *are* feelings – a mixture of remorse, embarrassment and regret – are mistakes only really mistakes if they come with the sinking feeling that follows? What if I told you that you could claim full autonomy over your mishaps, and that only YOU could decide if you'd actually failed at something?

I'm all too familiar with the feeling of failure. I've never won an award for any achievements in sport, or been recognised as

anything above average in academia. I dropped out of university after a year, but as it turned out, I'd failed the year anyway. I failed my theory driving test twice, and my practical test once. At 24, I had to quit my stressful 9 to 5 job and move back in with my parents for the sake of my mental health (and my finances). I started waitressing, which was perceived as a giant setback as I'd stopped waitressing at 19 to get on the corporate ladder; allegedly a sign of success, or something like that (plot twist: it isn't). I'm almost entirely unfazed about anything competitive and I wonder if it's because, after 27 years, I'm so used to the feeling of failing that I simply cannot comprehend the feeling of winning.

Existing on this planet under the label

means that, to many, I'll always have failed at fully attaining womanhood. As with all of my other shortcomings, I'm accustomed to hearing *'Not quite – nice try, though.'* If I've truly failed at womanhood, why does it also feel as though I've failed as a trans person by transitioning so seamlessly at an early age? If being trans is remarkable, as I effortlessly slip under the radar, am I unremarkable? A lot of the time, it certainly feels that way.

My biggest failures and mistakes have not been revolutionary – nobody died, and the sun rose the next day, as it always does. My 'failed relationships' never actually failed, because relationships aren't about winning, they're simply past encounters with people that turned out not to be right for me. Someone once told me that regardless of how long someone is in your life for, you always have something to teach them and if you're open to it, they have something to teach you, too. Whether things are good or bad, I try to see all my life experiences in this way. And with that, I realise that my failures are only as big as the feelings I experience around them. If failure is simply a feeling, and I abandon any shame around my shortcomings, is it possible that none of my failures in life have actually been failures – only experiences paired with feelings?

What if each of my failures were

stepping stones

instead? What if each blip, which at the time felt like tripping over a hurdle everyone else seems to glide over so effortlessly, was in fact a skydive with a landing that brought me to exactly where was best for me? In skydiving, nobody cares about the way someone falls; they marvel at the journey and the courage it took to jump in the first instance. What if, in life, we're never really competing against anyone, not even ourselves? What if I shunned the idea of failure because, as I've learned, it is truly impossible to fail at something if you do it authentically?

My breakthrough moment was 3 years ago, a time I sometimes refer to as 'my London meltdown.' I'd been struggling in a job that I found incredibly stressful, but sounded impressive to people when they asked me about it. I'd brag about the enormous responsibility I had and how well I was doing, *'even without a university degree!'* My parents essentially rescued me. The move back home felt like my biggest failure of all – doesn't everyone have their shit together already by the age of 24? Why am I opting for minimum wage and moving out of the city that holds all of my friends and all that my adult life knows for a full fridge and Sky TV? I now understand that accepting this help from my parents was one of the most effective forms of self-care I have ever undertaken.
In moving home, I hit reset.

As with every other supposed failure, I dusted myself down, and I started again.

As I write this in February 2021, we're fast approaching the 1-year mark of lockdowns in the UK. A year that has felt like a decade. In the past 12 months, after what had felt like 26 years of failure, I finally found a full-time occupation that is fulfilling, enjoyable and completely in alignment with all of my values. In June 2020 I started working for gender-free, vegan makeup brand and, at the start of 2021, I was promoted to Marketing Manager. I managed to move out of my family home and in with friends for the first time, start a relationship with someone who makes me feel appreciated and respected, and save enough money to put a deposit down on a flat if I want to. I also featured in a fragrance campaign for International Women's Day and am currently in a prime time TV advert. All during the pandemic, all while being trans, all while dealing with the traumas that comes with. If only I'd known during my teens that I'd go from daily bullying and a feeling of being endlessly misunderstood, to now always being undeniably true to myself and feeling valued and celebrated by everyone I choose to surround myself with.

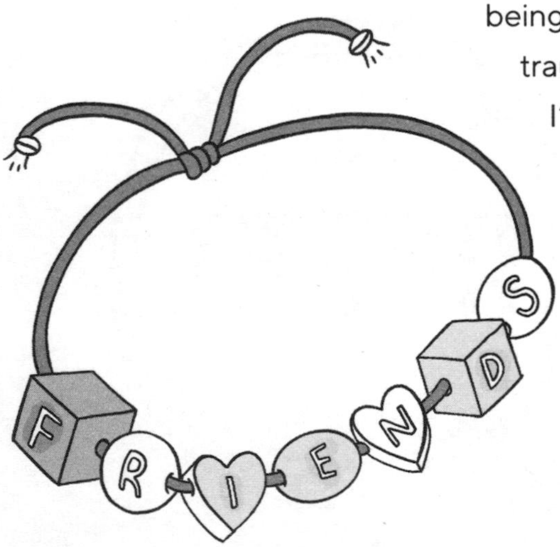

I recently read a quote about privilege; it said

YOU DIDN'T **MAKE** GOOD CHOICES, YOU **HAD** GOOD CHOICES.

and while it is beyond doubt that the privileges afforded to me (and there are many) will be benefiting me for the rest of my life, it still hasn't been easy – and against many odds, during this apocalyptic world, things have started to really happen for me. It took me 26 years to begin to feel at least a little bit settled. Twenty-six years of feeling as though I was missing out, or failing as everyone around me seemed to thrive. As I write this at 27 I'm very grateful to tell you that I'm reaping the rewards of inundated and undeniable success by my own standards – and nobody else's.

If you aren't getting yours right now, please know that this doesn't mean it'll never come. It will. Give it time, and don't measure it against anyone else's wins. Keep hope. Be sure to have only the best people around you who enrich your time and add value to your life. Easier said than done, I realise, but believe that you absolutely deserve the best and hold everyone around you to that standard. Most importantly, find what makes you happy. When you begin to chart your own path based on what'll bring you happiness, you set your wins and fails on your own well-being without them being dictated to you by anyone else.

In the words of Albert Einstein:

> *"If you judge a fish on its ability to climb a tree, it will live its whole life believing that it is stupid."*

Without the lows, there are no highs. Claim ownership of your failures and mistakes; read about them, share about them, and befriend them. Get to know them, and try not to be afraid of them. Also, never be afraid to hit reset when you can, and always accept support when made available to you. Next time you feel yourself failing, do it boldly. Hold your head high. Harbour no shame, puff out your chest, then take a bow. Remember to set your own bar

for failure, and move it if you need to. Realise that in life you'll have some lucky and not-so lucky moments, but in trying new things, stepping out of your comfort zone, and never being afraid to learn, you can create some of your own luck – and earn your own seat at the table. With each failure (I promise you) you are just one experience closer to getting to where you need to be.

Perhaps my one real failure in life has been in underestimating myself. So please believe me when I tell you that you already have all the strength you need within you to truly excel, and trust that when the time is right, you will.

10 TOP TIPS FOR BEING YOUR OWN CHEERLEADER

1

THINK POSITIVE!

I know that sounds cheesy as anything and something your mum might say, but on days where I've got up and told myself I'm going to have a great day and be productive as hell, weirdly enough that generally does happen! The art of 'manifesting' is really popular right now; the thinking behind it is that your positive thoughts can really help create your 'reality'. So try getting out of bed each day, looking in the mirror and saying to yourself:

'Today is going to be a good day'.

Put a message of positivity out into the universe and see what happens!

2

SAY YOUR ACHIEVEMENTS OUT LOUD (OR, BETTER STILL, WRITE THEM DOWN)

Think about the things that make you feel proud or happy, even
Think about the things that make you feel proud or happy, even just small things like getting a good grade on an essay or being helpful by emptying the (dreaded) dishwasher. When you get into bed each night, list – out loud or, even better, in a dedicated notebook – the things that made you feel GOOD about your day. Journaling like this is a great aid for your mental health. We all need to be reminded of what we've done well, and I find that when I see all the things I've achieved or that have made me happy that day written down on a page, I realise that my day has been better than I thought. Just try it and see.

3

NOURISH YOUR MIND & BODY

Eating good food and drinking plenty of water helps your body and your mind feel on top form. It is literally the fuel that keeps us going, otherwise we're running on empty like a car without petrol – and eventually we'll run out of gas and grind to a halt! Our bodies are made up of around 60% water, so when I feel tired, it's often because I'm dehydrated. Water keeps us hydrated which is vital for a sharp mind and a well-functioning body and BONUS, it can also help to give you super-glowing skin!

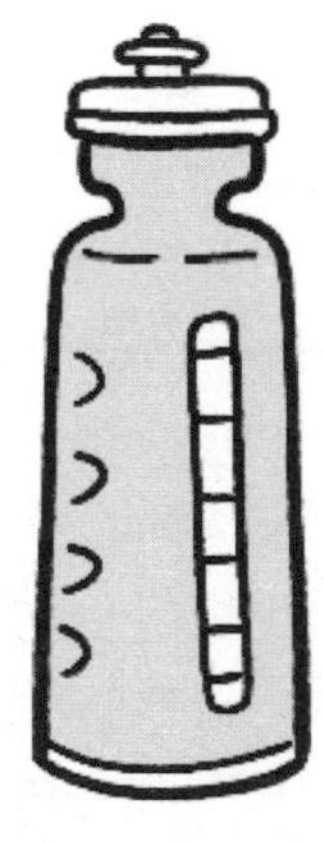

4

TAKE TIME OUT

Set aside some time for YOU – every day – even if it's just 30 minutes. Not only do you deserve it, but you also need it. Our lives are so fast-paced that having time to yourself is vital for your mental health. It's your life, and it's easy to forget sometimes that you're allowed to enjoy it. Treat yourself to half an hour of something that brings you pleasure, once a day. (And Netflix does count, yes!) For me, it's a long soak in the bath. Probably with Netflix on my phone precariously balanced on the side ...

5

LEARN TO SAY NO

Practise saying NO to things you don't want to do, be a part of or agree with. Unfortunately, it can still be a big thing for women to say no because we're taught to be amicable and to please. But screw that. Start setting your boundaries now, and people will be less likely to try to push them. When I first started saying no and standing up for myself, I would watch people get offended by it – until they realised it was me, growing up and taking control of my life. You can be in control of yours, too. So bring this powerful little word into your vocabulary!

6

SHARE YOUR WINS!

Be it earning good grades, making the sports team or landing a role in the school play, it's a lovely thing to share your achievements with others. You don't have to celebrate all on your own, or worse, push it down and not talk about it so you don't upset those around you. Real friends will always want the best for you and will cheer you on when you succeed!

7

CELEBRATE OTHER PEOPLE'S ACHIEVEMENTS

As women, I believe we should celebrate each other and lift each other up. And that goes for all women: your friends, your family, or other women you love and look up to! Because being happy for others makes it easier to be pleased for yourself when exciting things happen to you. And remember, just because something great happens to someone you know, it doesn't mean that something great won't happen to you. Your worth doesn't decrease because of someone else's success! So, let's boost each other up and delight in each other's achievements!

8

REST YOUR SLEEPY HEAD

This sounds a bit obvious I know, but my mood is usually in direct correlation to whether I've had enough sleep the night before. Did I stay up until 1am scrolling every app on my phone? Yes. Did I see lots of cute kittens and make up tutorials and can now contour my nose wonderfully? Yes. But, am I now incredibly tired and a bit grouchy because of it? Definitely, yes. Eight to 10 hours is the recommended amount of sleep for teens, so may I make a few sleep hygiene recommendations (and follow them myself!). I definitely get a better night's snooze on the evenings that I put my phone away at least an hour before my head hits the pillow. Blue light from phones has been shown to mess up your sleep-inducing hormones, so however enticing your phone is, try to switch off. As you know, I love a warm bath, which is good for sending me to the land of Nod, especially if I add an essential oil such as lavender or chamomile. Find what works for you and try to stick to a good nightly routine!

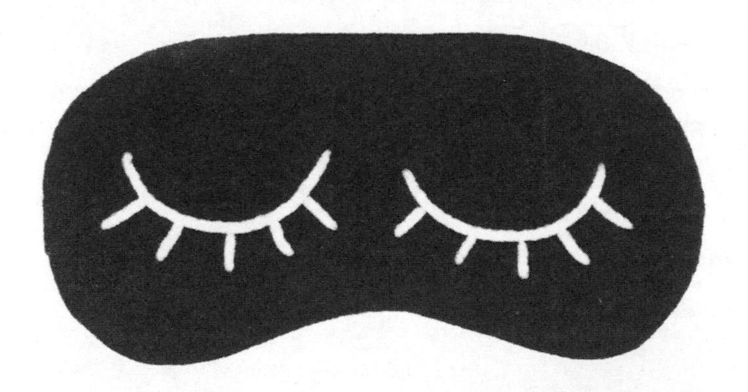

9
TREAT YOURSELF WITH KINDNESS

Be kind to YOU by imagining that you're rooting for your 6-year-old self. When I was 6, I was all gappy teeth, polka-dot skirts and I was really rather shy. Looking back at her now, I would hate her to hear some of the things I say to myself today. I would never berate 6-year-old me or get cross with her. I would encourage her and remind her of all the things she's great at, and let her know that she can achieve anything she wants to if she puts her mind to it. I'd like to make her proud. Our 6-year-old selves are still inside us, somewhere, so let's treat them with kindness.

10
BE PROUD OF YOURSELF

As a female, pride is an emotion we've been taught is unattractive. Have you ever had the feeling that, as girls and women, we are expected to receive compliments with coyness and humility? Well, proud warriors, let's battle that one and knock it to the ground! Next time someone says your hair looks great, your new dress is amazing or congratulates you on an achievement, don't look down and try and brush it off with embarrassment! No, look them straight in the eye and say

Thank you very much.

It takes practice, but trust me, you can get used to it!

STEP 2

A CALL TO ARMS

FRIENDSHIPS, FALLOUTS, SOCIAL MEDIA AND SPREADING KINDNESS

ATTENTION: This is a call to arms for anyone who is navigating this planet with the other 7 billion people on it. Gather your friends, gather your love interest, gather your granny – it's time to talk!

Picture this: I'm 18 years old, working in a foreign country, entirely on my own. On a day off, I took a trip to the beach, plonked myself down on the scorching hot sand and looked around. The waves were crashing in, families building sandcastles, groups of friends playing volleyball. It should have been an exciting time ... but instead I felt empty. Because as I sat there, on this golden beach with a blanket of perfect blue sky above me, I realised: I was all alone.

I was this small girl in a big new city, and without sounding like a film plot, I had no one.

It was in that moment that I realised how much I treasured the people in my life, and that life just wasn't fun without others to share it with; human connection may just be the most important thing of all.

Good friends are irreplaceable. Like pulling on a woolly jumper on a cold winter's day, a good friend can be like a warm hug just when you need it. There are friends you can get lost in the shopping mall with, who hold your hair back when you're sick, the ones you can sit in silence with and feel perfectly content. Of course, there are sometimes challenges and fallouts. Not everyone is destined to be in your life forever. I like to think of life as a big old story book: some people are there cover to cover, some just pop in for a chapter or a page, and some appear in chapter 2 and then rock back up in chapter 28 in an unexpected plot twist.

The same can be said for your first relationships; the most intense, topsy-turvy emotions that feel like you've swallowed a shooting star (but can implode and plummet to the Earth just as quickly!)

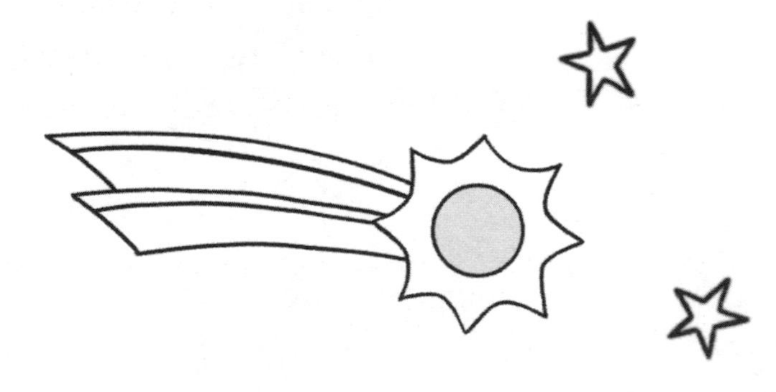

As the people around you shout 'You're too good for them' or 'There's plenty more fish in the sea', you're sat there crying to Olivia Rodrigo thinking ... but I liked that fish! Think of it like this: if anyone had the key to relationships there'd be fewer great heartbreak songs, so really it's something we all have to muddle through together.

A Call to Arms is also all about connection, to others, to ourselves, to the universe via social media and the problems that can sometimes arise. I promise there are no lectures on the perils of social media because that's not helpful nor is it real life. But from filters to followers and apps that are designed to connect us with others, there is a reminder here that social media can be your friend and your foe. So, be kind to yourself and others while on social media. It goes without saying that bullying online or IRL is Never. Ever. OK.

So it's time to rewire those negative thoughts, take that little mean voice and flick it off your shoulder, and gather a posse. While I firmly believe that a woman alone has the power to stage an Armageddon ... it's way more fun with a

supportive gang behind you!

"Fight for the things that you care about, but do it in a way that will lead others to join you."

RUTH BADER GINSBERG,
FORMER JUSTICE OF THE SUPREME COURT OF UNITED STATES

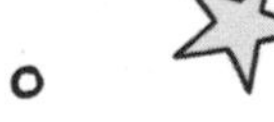

ON FEMALE FRIENDSHIPS: AN ODE TO MY BEST FRIEND, LAURA DONNELLY, ACTOR

On my first day of primary school, at the age of 5, I met my best friend, Bronagh. We argued with each other about who was going to play in the toy kitchen and then, somehow, in what must have been a remarkable feat of early maturity, or the work of a very clever teacher, we became friends. After that we were pretty inseparable.

We lived very near one another and would hang out both in and out of school. Every time I went to Bronagh's house I was greeted by her stuffed dog, Fred Astaire, landing on top of my head from two floors up. We were never girlie girls. We didn't play with dolls or do each other's hair. Instead, we set up a Secret Police Club in which we investigated the local cat lady for possibly being a witch and looked into other 'supernatural happenings' in the neighbourhood. We acted out scenes from *Baywatch* and played *Dungeons and Dragons*. In all, we were pretty geeky and tomboyish.

As we grew up, we got along with other girls from our all-female convent school but we were always slight misfits. We were obsessed with *Nirvana* instead of *Take That*, we dabbled in amateur witchcraft (perhaps brought on by our obsession with the film, *The Craft*) and, when we could, we embarked on our first tattoos and piercings. It wasn't always easy at school being that way, I'd say we were neither particularly popular nor unpopular, but we had our fair share of nastiness from other girls around us. Neither of us were naturals at sharing our feelings with each other, but we knew we had each other's backs. We had a silly, fun, easy friendship. We still do to this day – more than three decades on.

As time went on there were ebbs and flows to our friendship. Sometimes we'd be on different paths and see a bit less of each other, especially after we both left the school we shared. But we'd always find our way back to one another. I wasn't always great at spotting when she was having a tough time and I acted selfishly sometimes. When I think back I regret not always having the maturity to be a great friend but she was always accepting and always there..

As we've grown up we've discovered new depths to a mature friendship. We are always there to help each other, listen to each other, offer support where needed. We have allowed each other to change and to totally be ourselves. Neither of us is afraid of the other one's darker or harder moments. Neither of us ever needs to put on a brave face when things aren't going so well, and we celebrate one another's joys and achievements. I always feel relaxed in her company and completely myself.

That, to me, is what is wonderful about a great female friendship.

There doesn't have to be pressure to please each other all the time, to be each other's *everything*. All the little disappointments that can build up in a romantic relationship don't have to be there. There is, or should be, total freedom to be whoever you want to be, to go off and have experiences without that person, other very meaningful friendships and romances – with total acceptance and a promise to always be there for each other. There doesn't need to be drama – romantic relationships will certainly bring you enough of that – but female friendship means that you are accepted and loved you for exactly who you are, no strings attached. It is, or at least I think it should be, easy.

Nowadays, when Bronagh comes round to my house, we just catch up, order a take-out and watch some film we've both always adored. Still easy. We make plans to retire to a house by the sea in our old age and live out our last days like the two old aunts in the film, *Practical Magic*.

When my first daughter was born,
Bronagh trawled the depths of the internet to get her an exact replica of her stuffed dog, Fred Astaire. That daughter starts primary school later this year and I can only hope that on her first day she finds a 'Bronagh'.

After almost 35 years, our friendship is one of the things I am most proud of in my life. It tells me what I always suspected.

You don't have to have a ton of female friendships. Just one really good one.

MY TAKE ON FRIENDSHIPS & FALL OUTS, MIA MCKENNA-BRUCE, ACTOR

Growing up, you think friendships are forever.

You have your matching bracelets, your photo albums, your plans of living next door to each other and naming your children after one another ... and then, one day, the person you thought was your 'forever friend' isn't that person anymore. Maybe your friend has started replacing you or cutting you out? Maybe they said or did something awful? Or maybe it was a slower process of realising they constantly dragged you down and made you feel a bit shit about yourself? Or maybe you just became different people and slowly drifted apart..

There's no way of putting it lightly – friendship fallouts can be heartbreaking. I've had my fair share of fallouts; some were temporary and we came back stronger, others were fairly life-changing and, at the time, I couldn't see myself bouncing back from them.

But I did. And so can you.

However awful, you always come back from fallouts. And that old saying 'What doesn't kill you makes you stronger'? It's true! In fact, fallouts with friends can be the most invaluable life lessons you'll ever have. Why? Because you're forced to look at the reasons people do the things they do, and even *more* usefully, the reasons YOU do the things you do.

There are numerous reasons why friendships don't work out; human beings change and that's absolutely OK. But you need to know when it's time to walk away from a friendship and or relationship. After all, you become the energy you surround yourself with, so if someone is filling you with negativity, which is draining your spirit, you owe it to yourself (and them) to walk away from that friendship.

So here is my mini-guide to friendship fallouts and how to handle them:

1 First of all, decide what you want the ideal outcome to be. Are your problems fixable, or did they do something truly unforgivable? Or perhaps you've discovered that they are a bit of a 'toxic friend' who is simply not going to change?

2 Make a list of the reasons you feel the friendship ended and exactly how that friendship made you feel. Then look at the list objectively and ask yourself if you would want your sibling or another close friend treated in that way – and if that's someone you still want in your life.

3 If you still want to keep this person as a friend but acknowledge that some things need to change within the relationship, consider being the bigger person and apologizing for the rift, or at least reaching out. A lot of times relationship breakdowns come from a lack of communication. Be honest, explain your feelings. They are ALWAYS valid.

4 If they are someone worth having in your life they will want to work through these issues just as much as you do. And if they *don't* want to work it out, at least you know you did everything you could!

5 A lot more weight is given to romantic break-ups than friendship fallouts, but let me tell you, a break-up with a friend can be just as tough. You feel you've lost 'your' person, the one that you may have grown up with, have made childhood memories with, gone through some of your biggest life moments with. And this is the person who you would go to for support – so a break up with a friend can make you feel doubly alone and vulnerable.

6 Give yourself the time to GRIEVE. You need time to come to terms with your loss. This may sound dramatic but this is a vital part of the process and will help you in the long term, so let yourself wallow and don't just brush it off.

7 Don't try to formulate 'sides'. However tempting it may be to have mutual friends in your corner, the reality is this will end up hurting you more. In a friend break up situation, people might tell you what you want to hear, then go and say the exact same to your ex-friend.

8 Back your damn self. You don't need people to tell you who was right and who was wrong. Know that regardless of anyone else, this friendship was not healthy for you. The right people will come into your life and stay there without you having to convince them you were right! Trust in yourself that you are fully capable of creating real friendships and you deserve real friendships, no matter what your ex-friend may have made you believe.

9 Make sure you confide in (and invest in) your true friends and talk to them about what you're going through. Bottling up your feelings is never a good thing. Otherwise it's going to come out in future friendships or even to a stranger on the street that has somehow reminded you of your ex-friend. *(This is real by the way I absolutely did cry at a stranger for no apparent reason!)*

10 Getting closure can be a good thing if you are both on the same page, but sometimes it's not worth it. If an argument with a friend becomes nasty and looks like it might turn into a character assassination, just walk away. There's no point staying in the conversation to try to get the last word just to be an emotional punch bag. If you don't get closure then the best thing is to write them a letter, outlining every feeling you've ever felt towards them. Write it down. Then burn it. Then get back to some meditation on self-love and get to know your worth!

The thing is, I know hardly anyone who hasn't gone through a horrible friendship break-up. Do you know the famous quote 'Friends for a reason, friends for a season, or friends for a lifetime'? You grow, you change, you fall out, you (maybe) make up. It's all part of life.

This year, I've made friends with people who now feel like family, but I've also fallen out with people I never thought I'd have to live without. But I am OK. Every day, I get more OK. And I absolutely promise you, you will be OK too.

If you try to learn something valuable from every person you have a relationship with, that way, no matter what the outcome

you've always gained something ...

WHY BULLYING IS NEVER OK,
SARA PASCOE, COMEDIAN & WRITER

I've spent most of my prep time for this essay checking the above statement for loopholes. Surely if someone is a big-headed jerk, a bit of bullying is alright? Just to bring them down to a normal person's confidence level? Or what about if there was a tyrannical dictator creating havoc, surely his* citizens should get together for a bullying campaign? Calling the despot names and making fun of how he walks until he cries and agrees to a democratic election?

*Sorry to be sexist, of course, women can be tyrannical too. Live your dreams.

I don't want to sound dumb in some future time when we've all agreed as a species that bullying is mostly wrong, except as a last resort, to save lives or win the World Cup or something. But I've realised there's a reason that bullying is *never* ok, and it's not a moral 'Because it's not very nice' reason. It's about the bully. The aggressor, the instigator, the meanie – *they* are not OK. Bullying is not a thing OK people do.

I think if we're honest with ourselves we've all experienced both sides of this. I know I have, so let me share my shame.

I hated going to school. Generally, I was not liked, which is different to bullying, it's still shit and hurtful but you can't really do anything about it. But there was some bullying as well. There was a girl in the year above who would regularly rip my tights or knock a drink out of my hand or throw my bag onto train tracks or off the bus. I never fought back or asked her to stop. Another fun memory is of an older boy who called me

He'd make whinnying, neighing noises whenever I walked past (which I did anything I could to avoid). I'm aware these are low-level vendettas but their impact was large. I was always on alert for one of my 'enemies' around any corner, in any toilet or cloakroom. I often hid during break times to avoid conflict or 'attack'. I was diminished by my own fear and by pathetic-ness; some days I was so stressed and upset about what might happen that I didn't go into school at all.

The worst occurrence, the one that still gives me the sweats decades later, was an orchestrated trick: a love note from a boy saying he wanted to kiss me. There was hope in my heart as I rushed at lunchtime to a secret rendezvous on the tennis courts. A group of kids from my class waited, gleeful at my stupidity and arrogance: 'Who'd wanna kiss you, you ugly bitch?' I was punched in the face by a girl who often requests my Facebook friendship now that I'm on TV.

So I was socially disrespected and once or twice, assaulted. But I'm far more haunted by the times I bullied others. I remember once picking on a boy called Richard in my class. The teacher had left the room and I used this lawless time to push Richard off his stool and refuse to give it back. He was a shy person and gentle, an easy target. I claimed he'd get the stool back if he did and said as I instructed. Then, like some mafia boss in school uniform, I had him hopping and dancing for me and giving me compliments. I humiliated Richard. I remember people laughing and I remember feeling accepted, superior, socially safe.

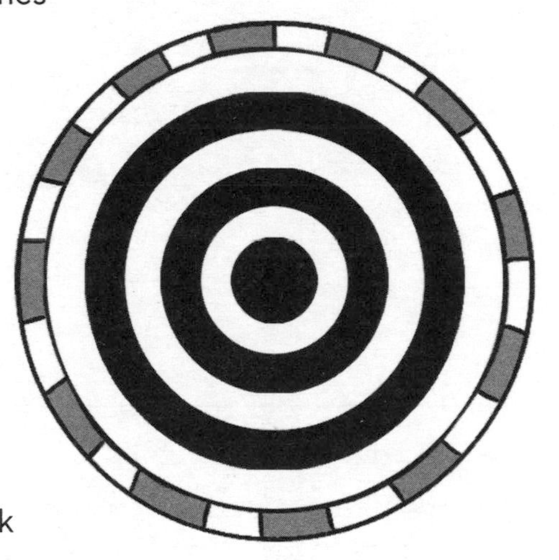

I feel sick about having behaved that way but I've admitted it so that you trust what I say next. Having been the bully and experienced this first-hand, I promise that whatever the approach or tactics of a bully, their aim is to feel less weak. For an unpopular weed like myself, making a victim of somebody else gained me respite and a fleeting sense of strength. By oppressing and pushing others down it is possible to feel that you are rising. This happens plenty in the adult world too, unfortunately; in workplaces, in gossipy social media chats, in families and even in relationships. The truth about the human ape is that sometimes we behave like apes, and it's nasty.

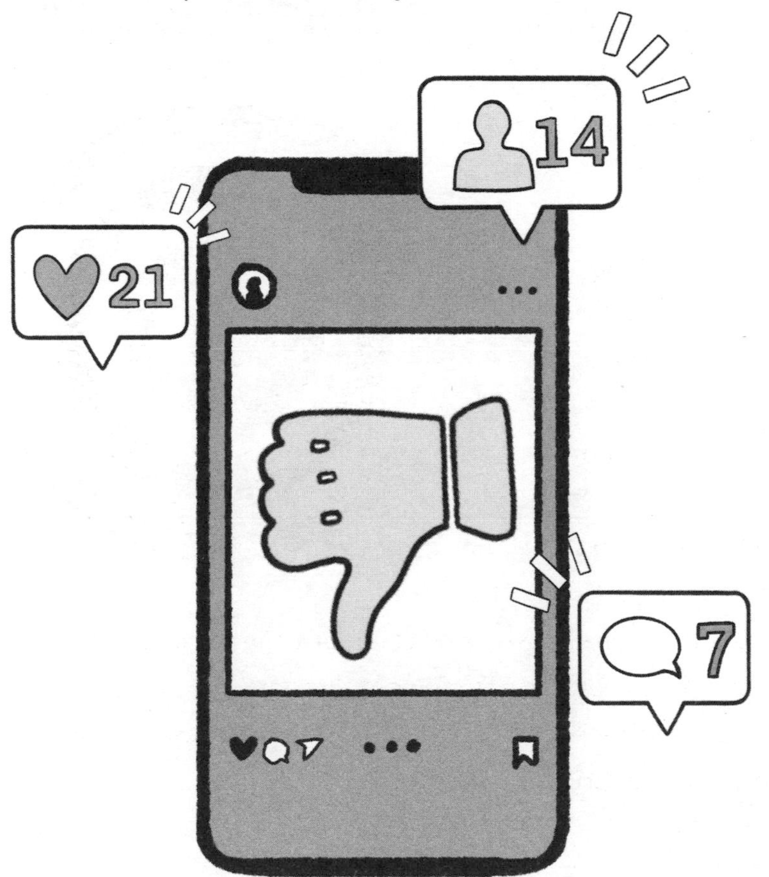

Social status is very important to all apes (including you and me). We can't switch it off or intellectualise our way out of it

because it's hardwired by evolution into our bodies, into our limbic system and hormonal responses. It feels *bad* to be low-status, disrespected, ignored and/or belittled. Conversely it feels GREAT to be high-status, respected, celebrated, popular and/or loved. This is because, in evolutionary terms, the latter translates to more resources, more potential for mates, more protection and increased safety. It literally means a better life, something we all want.

There is a 'constructive' way of attaining this – building up yourself and your skills and your friendships until you feel glorious and satisfied.

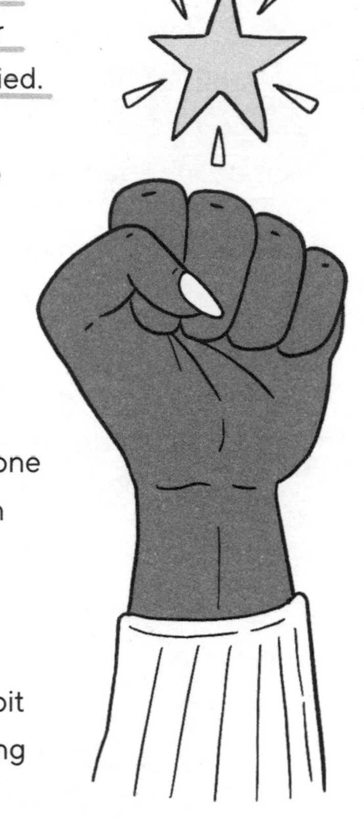

And there is a 'destructive' path, one where you belittle others with the aim of raising yourself. Perhaps your work colleagues will be scared of you; perhaps your friends will always let you have your own way and perhaps you'll interpret this as some mighty power? I'm not going to argue that one approach is morally superior here (although it is), but one is better. Would you rather be a towering actual thing, like an oak tree or a roomy mansion or a massive horsey face horse? Or a hole that stuff falls into – just a pit in the ground, tripping people up and getting in everyone's way?

Now whenever I feel the temptation to demean someone, I interpret this as a warning signal. It still happens more than I would like, an urge to snap or squash, a sense of how easy it would be to just ... these thoughts are the alarm bells for my own insecurity.

If I was feeling confident in my own ability, work ethic, and the effort I've put in, why would I want to undermine someone else?

When the little bully inside me pops her head up, that's a sure sign I'm feeling small and weak. Recognising that means I can concentrate on what I need to do to feel stronger. Introspection, journaling, therapy, *Ru Paul's Drag Race* – anything except taking somebody else's stool.

I'm quite regularly not OK, but as long as I don't take it out on others, then that's OK.

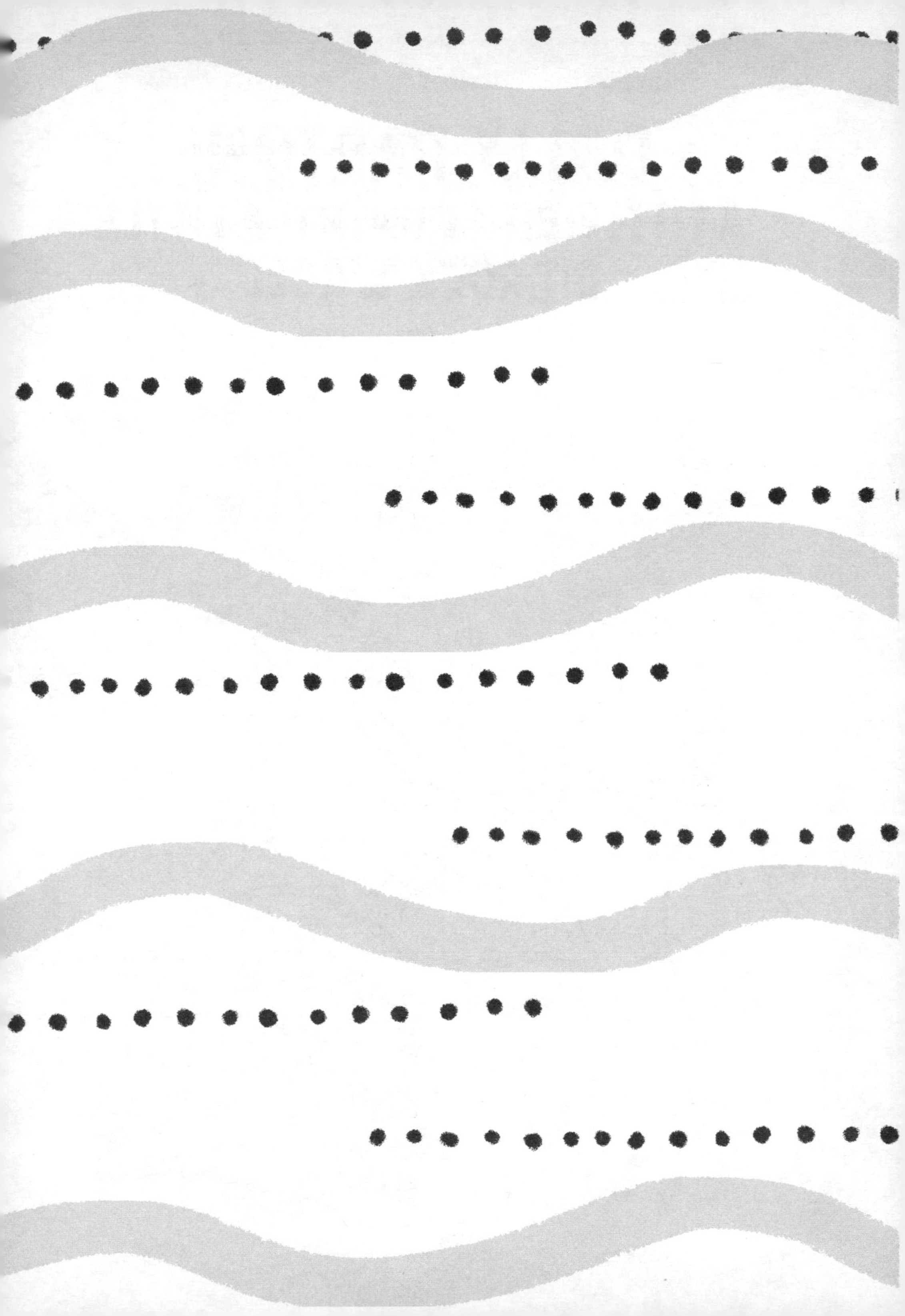

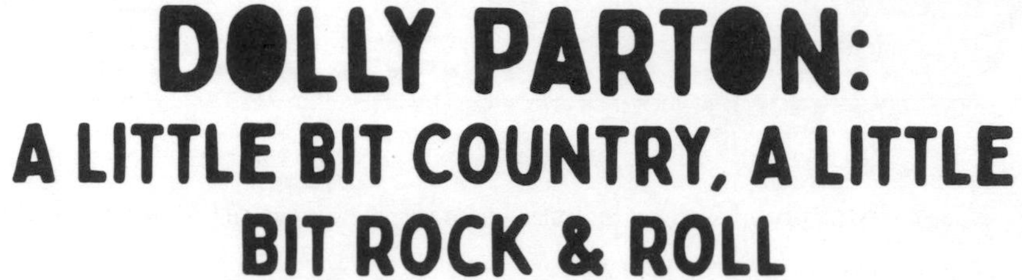
DOLLY PARTON:
A LITTLE BIT COUNTRY, A LITTLE BIT ROCK & ROLL

'You'll never do a whole lot unless you're brave enough to try.'

Who doesn't love Dolly Parton? A living legend of country music who has stolen the hearts of country music fans for over sixty years! Quite officially a legend, too, as in 2004 the US Library of Congress gave her the prestigious Living Legend Award (how's that for a social media bio?).

She's ruled the radio waves since the age of 13, and continues to be one of the most celebrated female bosses in the music industry today. Not only that, Dolly is an icon for the LGBTQ+ community and is celebrated by women worldwide as a feminist icon who proves you can rule the world while wearing a bit of sparkle. Oh, and Dolly is also one of an elite group of people to receive at least one nomination at the Emmys, Grammys, Oscars, and Tonys.

But the most important thing that Dolly is known for?

Her kindness.

From her humble beginnings in the mountains of East Tennessee where she shared a single room with her 11 brothers and sisters, Dolly has never forgotten her roots, and works tirelessly to help others. In 1986 she set up The Dollywood Foundation and began offering college scholarships to high school students from all over the US to encourage them to further their education.

In 1991 Dolly launched the Buddy Program that encouraged teens to pair up and sign a contract to agree that they both must

graduate. If they did, they would both receive $500. The Buddy Program caused the class drop-out rate to plummet to 6% for the students who took part, and provided a bit of a kick-start for young students.

But like all good Country song writers, Dolly believes in the power of a good story and, in 1995, she set up Dolly Parton's Imagination Library, a programme that gifts books to children, to inspire in them a love of reading. Each month the children enrolled in the programme receive a free book in the post. Today it has sent out over a whopping 100 million books. Not only that, Dolly also has a YouTube channel where she reads bedtime stories to children!

Dolly is loved around the world, not just for her talent but for her huge heart. A kind act will never be wasted. So every day (and not just from 9 to 5, ha ha!)
we should all aim to

A guitar is not necessary
(but you do you!) but just
with the intention to
make the world a better place!

SOCIAL MEDIA: FRIEND OR FOE?
KOSAR ALI, ACTOR

So – and please tell me I'm not the only one who does this – I have to admit I woke up this morning, and the first thing I did was go online and scroll past fancy cars, huge mansions with these amazing coastal views, and beautiful women wearing garms I could never afford, lol. Then, I went on to obsessively study videos of totally addictive dance routines and 60-second reels of absolute nonsense. It's become a bit of a habit, you know. It's like I've made this subconscious decision that I HAVE to do this every morning. Occasionally, I might get up and run to the toilet, BUT, somehow (inevitably), I find myself scrolling even while on the loo!

Now don't get me wrong, this is not always a bad thing, but there has to be a balance, right? Social media can either be your friend or your foe, and of course why wouldn't we want to harness its power so that it becomes almost like our digital best friend? Social media is a world of its own with celebrities, influencers, artists, gamers – all types of people – all occupying the same universe. It can be incredible. However, when you start looking at some of these people and their fantastic lifestyles, seeing everything they have, that you don't have – you might start comparing yourself to them ...

No, No, No. That's where we stop ...

So I created this little list that I look back on when I started to feel overwhelmed by the power of social media. I often refer to it to remind me that SM should be my friend, and as such, it should not be sapping my spirit or making me feel down ... So let's have a look at my 3-point SM checklist:

1 COMPARISON IS THE THIEF OF JOY

Let's face it, it's hard not to compare ourselves to others. I'd be lying if I said I don't do it at all. However, make it a rule not to compare yourself to anyone, but especially on social media. Why? Because you are beautiful, talented and unique, that's why. There is literally no one like you in this world and that's so magical. Also remember that everything you see on social media isn't necessarily the truth; you only see a version of what you've been allowed to see, from photo filters, images edited to 'perfection' and staged shoots.

But nothing in life is perfect! There are no standards you need to live up to!

It's true – there are some mean-spirited people who hang out online but usually they're struggling with something themselves, and sadly, being mean is the way they deal with their own issues. We all have different upbringings, backgrounds, hobbies and talents. And we all react in different ways to content we see, hear or read online. But I would suggest thinking hard about what your own personal 'triggers' are for social media content and AVOID THEM AT ALL COSTS.

Press

on those accounts that make you feel bad, and hit

Follow

on those that inspire, motivate and make you feel positive. Believe me, there are so many! And finally, remember that YOU are YOU, so you celebrate yourself and your life – not some curated version of reality you see online!

2 WHO CARES ABOUT LIKES AND FOLLOWERS?

OK, when I used to post something online, I'd find myself obsessively checking my phone, (sometimes literally every 30 seconds) to see how many likes and followers I'd gained. Yep, I was hooked on the dopamine hit of 'likes'. All this without knowing that what I was actually doing was seeking reassurance and validation from people in a virtual world that mostly I didn't even know! Before long, it began to affect my perception of myself and how I felt on a daily basis.

We all use social media for different reasons. Perhaps you are a maker or artist and sell or promote your products that way? Perhaps you enjoy creating a grid that looks aesthetically pleasing? Perhaps you like to keep distant (or close!) friends and family updated on what you're up to? Perhaps you use SM as a way of curating memories, a bit like a keepsake album of all the good times?

So have a good think about why you post online and, I say, just enjoy posting for YOU, regardless of how many likes, comments and new followers you get. If you want to post your own content do it at your own pace in your own time, and never be afraid to be authentically you.

Post what you want to, not what you think others want to see, and don't let anyone make you feel uncertain of yourself or what you do.

THE POWER IS ALL YOURS!

And like a good friend, SM should never take advantage of you ...

3 YOU ARE IN CONTROL!

In this crazy time we're living in we are exposed to

So.
Much.
Information.
And.
Content!

And social media can help to make that feel really overwhelming at times.

But I'm here to remind you that, actually, YOU are in full control of what you want to receive and what you don't. I only follow the social media accounts of people whose content I enjoy; those who make me laugh and feel good. I ban or restrict certain words, phrases, pictures or content that I don't want to see, and I set myself a time limit for being online, which allows me to decide how much of my day I will spend on social media. Sometimes it's 30 minutes in the afternoon and 30 minutes in the evening, or sometimes it's only weekends and not weekdays. You get to decide, but make sure you always put your mental wellbeing first.

So, my fellow Digital Doubters, I hope my 3-point checklist might help and encourage you to build some guidelines and boundaries around social media. Trust me, I wish I had created them much earlier. Always remember that social media should NEVER have the power to make you feel less than you are. No one else thinks like you, acts like you, talks like you OR has talents like you. Embrace your individuality. And make sure that social media stays your friend and does not become your foe ...

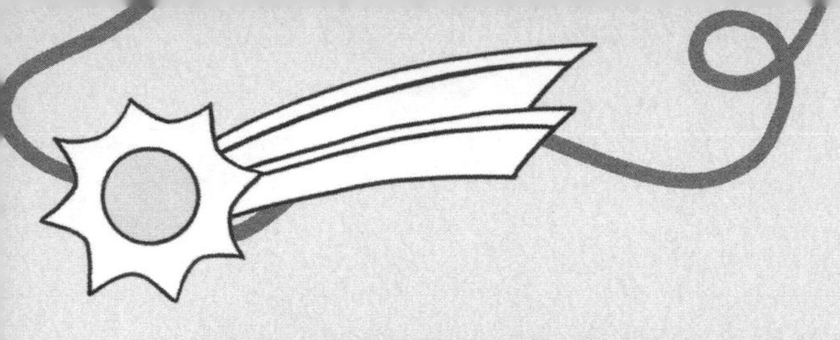

PEER PRESSURE, CHARLOTTE JORDAN, ACTOR

Howdy. Hello. Hi. My name is Charlie. I'm not a therapist, I'm not a psychologist, and I ain't gonna lie to you, I didn't even make it to college; the only thing that qualifies me to talk to you about this topic are the experiences I had myself as a teenage girl.

So this is a collection – albeit a fairly waffly one – of my thoughts on the things that peer pressure taught me, because looking back now I would regard the scenarios I found myself in due to peer pressure as educational. It taught me a lot about myself and it taught me a lot about boundaries. Knowing your boundaries means you know what you are comfortable with and, more importantly, *un*comfortable with. Learning about your boundaries helps figure out what your values and beliefs are as an individual. Even if they change as you grow older, this is something to try and embrace because they help define who you are, all the way into adulthood. So shall we dive in?

Though pressure can come in many forms – from your family, your teachers, maybe even yourself – I feel strongly that *peer pressure* is in a league of its own. Bad news: it can't be escaped. You can run but you can't hide. Sorry, 'tis inevitable. Every single human will have felt it at some point, in some way.

But there is a silver lining: you are not alone. Huzzah.

Good(ish) news: I'd like to say peer pressure disappears at approximately 'this age', at 'this time' but I don't think it does. Instead it sort of evolves into a different type of pressure. Societal pressures creep in and people want to know why you aren't planning your wedding or your 2.5 kids in your mid-twenties blah, blah, blah ... but that's a different topic for a different time.

My point is, what changes is you and your capability to deal with it. Even if you still feel that same echo of peer pressure when you're older you are more settled in who you are. You are more confident. If what you want and what you like are a little bit different you're able to speak up and use your voice without the fear of being penalised or ostracised for it. And without sounding like a cushion your lovely Nana has knitted, it comes from self-acceptance and self-love.

You are on your own journey, you'll do things when you're good and ready and if people don't like it, they can lump it.

Flicks hair.

Now's probably a good time to make it clear that, I absolutely did not have this debonair attitude towards peer pressure during my own teenage experiences. No, Sir. I was never considered particularly 'cool' at school. I use quotation marks because I want to try and drill into you the fact that your aim shouldn't ever be to be perceived as 'cool'. It's a fashion word and like fashion it's ever-changing. What's cool one minute isn't cool the next. My advice would be to find things that make you *happy.*

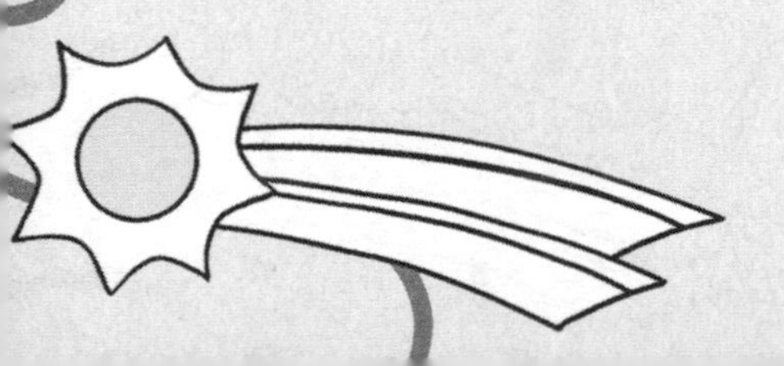

Whatever music, whatever clothes, whatever hobbies bring you a bit of joy are the things you should stick to regardless of what is currently considered to be 'cool'.

Around the age of 13, when Queen B of my year group and her herd of cronies were singing the latest hippest, new rap song (I know now the song was in fact Flo Rida's *Low,* at a time when I was all 'Flo who? Apple what now?') they made fun of me because I had never heard of it nor the rapper who wrote it. They tried to make me rap a verse knowing full well I wouldn't know where to start. I stood there looking between the floor and the ceiling while they laughed and proceeded to shout things like

'Stupid Penguin!'

and

'Why don't you ever know this stuff, Penguin!'

Side note, let me explain 'Penguin'...

I was really into ballet from the age of 10 to 15. I took it very seriously and loved it deeply. With a serious ballet obsession comes many, many hours of training after school. I was soon known as the ballet girl who 'walked weird' due to constantly training my body to be turned out. This 'turn out' extended into my daily walk and made me waddle a bit like ... yes, indeed, ... a penguin. It's funny to me now but at the time it made me want to dig a deep hole and bury myself alive.

I'd like to say in response to the heckling I threw a sensationally witty and confident retort in their direction, which ended in their respect and (finally) their approval, but I did no such thing. I ran away and cried in the girls' loos for a solid 9 minutes, cursing my non-diversified taste in music (Britney, 'N Sync and the soundtrack to Andrew Lloyd Webber's hit musical *Cats* were all I cared to know).

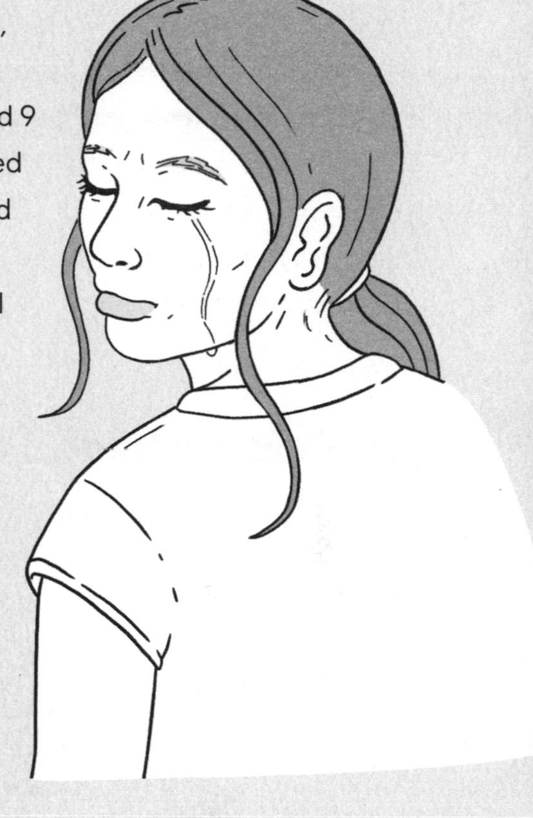

I went home and learnt *Low* with an almost wild aggression but it, sadly, didn't fill me with the same joy as belting out *Memories* from *Cats*. I learnt the rap genre isn't really for me but at least the next time they burst into song at lunch I could quietly join in and not feel like a weirdo. So I do understand the pressure to conform, and pushing a music boundary is not a big deal. It's a soft topic. But as you get further into teenage-dom you may be confronted with harder and darker topics.

Drinking. Smoking. Sex. Drugs.

What do you do when you find yourself in a situation where you're pining for the 'cool kids' acceptance but the only way to get it is by doing things you know deep in your soul you don't want to do. And Lord have mercy, you guys are tackling that along with tools and weapons of social media.

All I can say is if you find yourself in any situation where you feel that horrible knot forming in your stomach, listen to it and

don't feel obliged to try anything you aren't ready for.

Your teens are the time you start exploring and discovering things. You are given perhaps a small taste of independence for the first time. I was made fun of for not getting drunk, for not going to

loads of parties, for not getting with loads of boys. I remember vividly the first time I was told to try a cigarette.

GO ON.

Everyone's doing it.

It's not even a big deal.

What I wanted to shout is

'ACTUALLY IT IS A BIG DEAL, HELEN. IT STINKS AND THEY QUITE LITERALLY TURN YOUR INSIDES BLACK **EXCUUUUSE** ME FOR NOT WANTING TO SLOWLY KILL MYSELF WHILST SMELLING LIKE TRASH.'

But you know, there was no chance I felt ready to isolate myself further from my peers with that kind of outburst, so you are welcome to use what I used every time I found myself in a dodgy situation. Mum. Blame mum. Or whatever guardian figure is in your life. Every single time. She/He/They won't mind. My mum was the coolest but if you asked my school peers she was the lamest. She stopped me trying all sorts.

'I would but my mum would go mental and I don't feel like being grounded for four months. She's always watching.' God bless you, mum. And to this day I prefer leading a pretty quiet lifestyle. I don't smoke, I don't drink huge amounts, I didn't do anything major before I felt ready and I'm so, so glad.

Circling back to things like social media – I wasn't sure whether to broach this topic but I think the reason I stood my ground with my boundaries on sexuality as a kid was because my mum spoke to me about it like I was an adult, an equal and I'd like to continue that. No, we didn't have socials in my day but we did have camera phones and there was always some arsehole trying to get us to send nude pics 'just for him'. I can tell you now they aren't 'just for him'; he's showing all his friends and bragging about it to anyone who will listen. If you find yourself in this, or any scenario where you feel you're being sexually pressured by the person you like most, you mustn't do these types of things to feel desirable. Your body is precious and it is YOURS. If you want to share it with whomever you're into, he/she/they should earn your trust and respect.

If they're making you feel 'like a baby' for not doing certain things that's fiiine. Cry like one. Loudly in their face and then tell them to do one because they aren't the person for you. The type of person who's earned this kind of access to you would never want to rush you or make you do something you might look back on one day and regret.

I'm an actress. In my industry, it seems to be normal that we're asked to get our kit off for work or agree to do nudity before we've even auditioned for a part. I was in a position where I'd been offered a role but they didn't show me the true content of the script until I'd accepted the part. There were gratuitous scenes of a sexual nature I was unprepared for and I didn't appreciate the way Production blindsided me. I was an adult yet I felt the same way I did as a teenager, and even though my instinct is to people-please, I had to remind myself to speak up. And I was broke at the time, I ***really*** could have done with the income but I had to think if this was something I really wanted to do and use my voice to say actually, this isn't for me. It's an example of how peer pressure evolves as you mature and I hope you never feel the need to do something you're unhappy about just to satisfy somebody else.

It's also important to say it's not all stressful and scary. Some peers might turn into lifelong friends. Some pressure will be in the form of encouragement to work harder at the things you want to achieve. The right peers will bring new ideas, new experiences, new opinions on the big and little decisions you'll make. Should I get a fringe? (The answer 79% of the time is no). Should I commit to this or that for my exams? They'll listen to you, they'll support, they'll empathize. If you find the right sort of peers that help discover who you are and what you value in the right way, then hold on tight to them, because I know when you're a teenager your highs feel euphoric and your lows feel like they'll last forever but (spoiler) I promise they won't.

BUILDING THE KINDNESS HABIT, SHAHROO IZADI, BEHAVIOURAL CHANGE SPECIALIST

'What on Earth are you wearing?'

'You shouldn't be eating that!'

'Have you thought about losing some weight?'

In one way or another, these messages made up a huge part of my adolescent soundtrack.

Whether it was from kids at school, doctors or films and TV shows, I became aware pretty quickly that the size of my body was something I should be ashamed of or something that needed to be dealt with if I was to lead a happy life. It was clear that in order to be both attractive and taken seriously, I needed to find ways to make myself *smaller* as quickly as possible.

And so I tried ...

And I can report that it certainly wasn't difficult to find 'miracle plans' aimed at punishing and 'fixing' myself. At the age of 11, I started dieting. I obsessively educated myself on calories, took weight loss pills and jumped on the scales every morning. That is, until I couldn't bear it any longer. Then, I would eat everything I could get my hands on; it's no wonder really, I was starving, and before I'd even hit my teens I had already put food into 'good' or 'bad' categories

SPOILER ALERT: the 'bad' ones were the delicious ones.

Over time, I learned that the food binges served me in more ways than simply relieving hunger. They would, at least for a while, quieten my cruel internal soundtrack. Although they made me feel physically sick and like I had a hangover the next morning, they enabled me to escape the unkindness in the world (and in my own head) when it came to bodies like mine, and my inability to understand or accept myself as I was.

Then, because of everything I knew about diets, bingeing became the only way to quieten the *guilt* about bingeing, and so for years, I repeated the same vicious cycle: binge out of hunger and deprivation when I couldn't keep up another restrictive diet, feel weak and guilty because I had binged and 'undid' all my 'good work'; binge again so I could stop feeling that way for a bit, embark on another miracle cure that made my breath smell, hair fall out and brain fog up, and binge again because I was starving ... And so it went on.

I assumed that any attempt at changing my habits (eating or otherwise) had to be punitive and that I deserved to suffer for being so weak. I also assumed that my life wouldn't really start until I looked different.

I was on high alert for guidance on what was okay for people who looked like me and what we could do to change it. I mentally noted everything people said about women with bodies like mine. How they should eat less, hide their bodies and be embarrassed to take up space in every possible way.

I was always listening out for the most gruelling way possible to change my behaviours, both when it came to food and, indeed, any other area of my life. After all, I assumed that the meaner you were to yourself, the better the results.

Boy, was I wrong.

Eventually, in my twenties, I found myself sat in front of a counsellor telling them that I disliked my body, hated food and felt totally out of control. But it was a turning point for me because from that point on, I began a process of *unlearning*, starting with unpacking my beliefs about women, diets and body image.

At the same time, was working as an assistant psychologist in addiction treatment and realised how much I had in common with people who felt powerless over their habits. I noticed that the techniques that were helping people to transform their lives and break a cycle of ingrained habits were completely different to the things I'd tried throughout my life. These techniques focused on building strong foundations of self-kindness, self-awareness and self-belief. They weren't about punishment, but forgiving yourself and understanding *why* you'd developed the habits you had.

I began to entertain the possibility that being horrible to myself wasn't only something I didn't deserve, it was also an approach that wasn't helping me change my behaviours in any area of my life. What came next was nothing short of a transformation in every possible way. I shifted my focus from how I looked and what I weighed, to how I felt and what I deserved.

Cut to today and I write books about habit-change and share what I wish I'd known when I was younger; that self-kindness is not only what we deserve, it's key to building – and embedding – new behaviours.

So when it comes to forming new habits, this is my formula for showing yourself the ultimate kindness:

Believe in your capacity to spontaneously make decisions that you'll be happy you made tomorrow. Plans are great, but you need to trust *yourself* more than your plans; not least as the only guarantee is that your plans won't always go to plan.

Forgive yourself quickly! Whether you've dropped your keys and find yourself locked out or replied to a 'tricky' message without giving it enough thought, learn from it and try to forgive yourself as quickly as you would a loved one. Not just because you deserve the same consideration, but because beating yourself up about one thing for too long can spiral into unhelpful thinking and is a waste of time in the pursuit of your meaningful goals.

Take the advice you imagine the wisest person you know would give you when faced with a difficult choice.

Become your own cheerleader when you need a pep talk. You have a 24-hour coach right there; one who knows exactly what you need to hear when you're doubting yourself. Choose to develop a helpful soundtrack and *everything* becomes easier.

Focus on the feeling you're moving towards, not the one you're moving away from. Change isn't about shedding negatives, it's about getting excited about creating a life of purpose that you're proud of and enjoy.

Reflect on your strengths and achievements in moments of self-doubt. Whenever you want to create a new habit, don't focus on what's 'wrong' with you. Instead focus on your strengths and the resources you have at your disposal, and consider how staying the same is actually serving you.

Treating urges, cravings and triggers as alerts, not commands. YOU get to decide to put a space between *wanting* to do something and actually doing it.

Make self-care unconditional. Don't wait to reward yourself with enjoyable things simply when you've 'earned' them. Whether it's lighting a scented candle, wearing your bright-coloured dungarees or asking for fair and equal pay or treatment, you deserve to enjoy those things now. Plus, when you give yourself signals all day that you – and your quality of life – matter, then it becomes easier to slot in new kinder habits.

Make the same decisions for your body and mind that you'd want the person you love most to make for theirs – every day, at every opportunity.

Finally, always remember: change is difficult. But developing self-kindness makes it a lot easier to do difficult things!

10 TOP TIPS FOR FINDING YOUR PEOPLE

1 CHOOSE WISELY

It's a widely held belief that you are a combination of the five people you spend the most time with. Which, if you're surrounded by the right people, is a great thing! But it's also why choosing the people you surround yourself with is so important! So, let's fill our lives with positive, life-affirming friendships, people who make us feel good, who we genuinely love spending time with and make life more enjoyable!

2 IT'S OK TO LET GO!

That being said, it's good to know when to let go. Negative relationships can bring us down and have no place in your life. People who talk behind each other's back, deliberately cause fights, or put others down are not the people you want around. Once upon a time I had a friend who was incredibly possessive of me, who didn't want me having any other friends and would try to isolate me from others by telling them untrue things. Once I figured out what was happening, I said 'adios' and found myself an amazing group of five girlfriends who always had each other's back.

3 ASK FOR WHAT YOU WANT

Don't be afraid to ask for what you want or need from friend. I'm not talking about material things, but emotional. If you need support after, say, a fallout, break-up or parental dispute, or need a laugh because you're feeling a bit down – tell them! We sometimes expect people close to us to just know how we feel, but human beings are not psychic, so reaching out and explaining your emotions can be really useful. A good friend will do the same for you. Me and my best friend often say

"I need a laugh. Send dogs."

And send each other endless videos of cute dogs doing stupid things when the other is feeling down.

BUILD EACH OTHER UP 4

As friends it's important to be each other's biggest champions! Which means avoiding people who try to belittle your ambitions and goals. Growing up, I was on TV sometimes, and not everyone was always supportive about it. Some people would make mean comments, or put me down, and I'd feel really hurt. But I knew acting was what I loved, and what I wanted to do as an adult, so the good-hearted souls around me used to remind me not to let those people and their negative thoughts win.

Because we have to build each other up, not tear each other down.

5

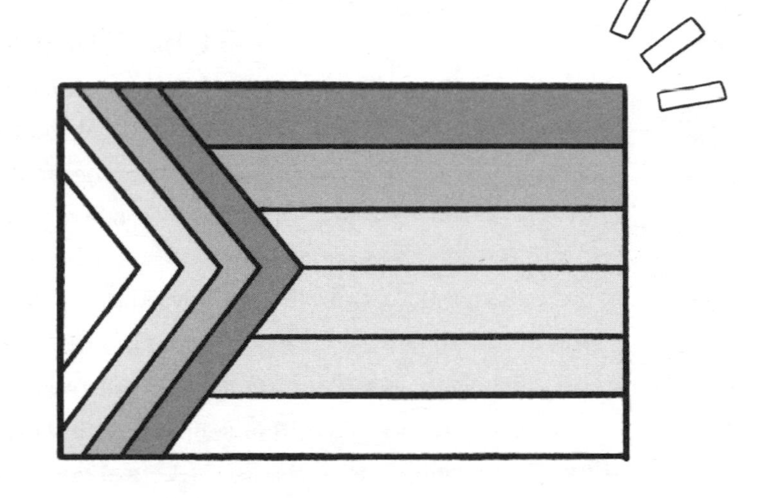

MAKE A STAND

Look out for people whose morals align with yours. This is not to say you have to agree on everything, you don't, people with different opinions make life more interesting. But do they stand for the same things as you? Do they think bullying is wrong? Are they passionate about equality or saving our planet? When it comes to morals, my friends and I, are all very similar. We think loyalty is key, are always standing up for women's rights, we support the LGBTQ+A community wholeheartedly and always aim to be as inclusive as possible to everyone we meet. There are still some things we disagree on, but that's more to do with which episode of *Friends* is our favourite ...

FIND YOUR TRIBE 6

So how do you find your people if they are not sitting next to you in classes every day? Think about what activities you enjoy, what shared interests you could have with other people? Do you love reading (I want to say yes, seeing as you're here, reading this!) so can you join a book club? Do you love sport? If so, get involved with a local athletics/football/netball team! Do you love drama? Look for a local youth theatre. I spent many nights a week in dance class, and the girls I met there were some of the kindest, most wonderful friends I have ever had. We bonded over our love of dance, and it was always so refreshing to have friends outside school!

7 DITCH THE JUDGE

'Don't judge a book by its cover' is an oldie but a goodie. When we first meet people we're often quick to form an opinion of them, without properly getting to know them. I once had a friend who, on the outside, was incredibly loud and came across as very confident. As someone who is quite shy, when I first met her I was intimidated by her gregarious personality, but as we got to know each other, I realised that 'confidence' was just her surface attitude, and underneath was a super-smart, sensitive young girl. It's important to give people chances, let them into your life and see how you get along, the same way you'd want people to give you a chance when they meet you.

And it's OK to argue sometimes. We shouldn't write people off after one fight, but try and see both sides of an argument. And

it's important to recognise you're in the wrong and apologise – and equally to know when you deserve an apology.

Open and honest discussions are so important. Sometimes people make you feel bad unintentionally, so it's important for friends to share when they're hurt, even when those conversations are a little harder.

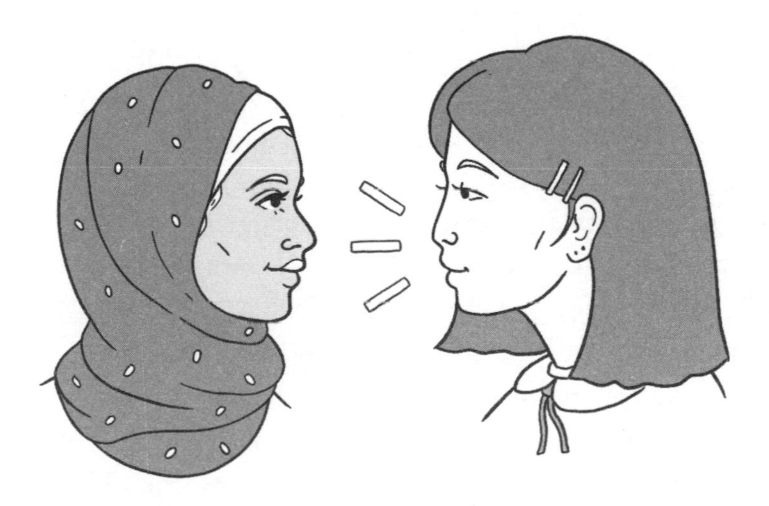

9 TALK TO STRANGERS

Hear me out, I know this goes against everything your mum taught you! But in safe, social settings, it's great to know how to start up a conversation and make a new friend. You might even learn a new thing or two! I find this concept terrifying. Nothing scares me more than having to walk into a room of strangers and talk to them!

So when I do this, I 'pretend' I'm someone else, someone much more confident and outgoing. Don't overthink it if you say something weird or silly, or if the person doesn't reply how you thought they would. Not everyone will be for you, a hard lesson to learn in life is that not everyone is going to 'get' you, but it's still a good skill to have to help you find your tribe.

MAKE A DIFFERENCE TOGETHER 10

Try to find people who are making a difference. Friends who have learnt from experiences will share their stories and will leave a positive footprint in their life and yours. The ones who want and are willing to help others are always good to be around. When I started working for the charity Stem4, and met the amazing women on their mission to help teenage mental health, it had a profound effect on me. Suddenly it gave things a bit more of a purpose, knowing I could be a part of something that genuinely helped people.

Sometimes helping others, also helps ourselves.

STEP 3

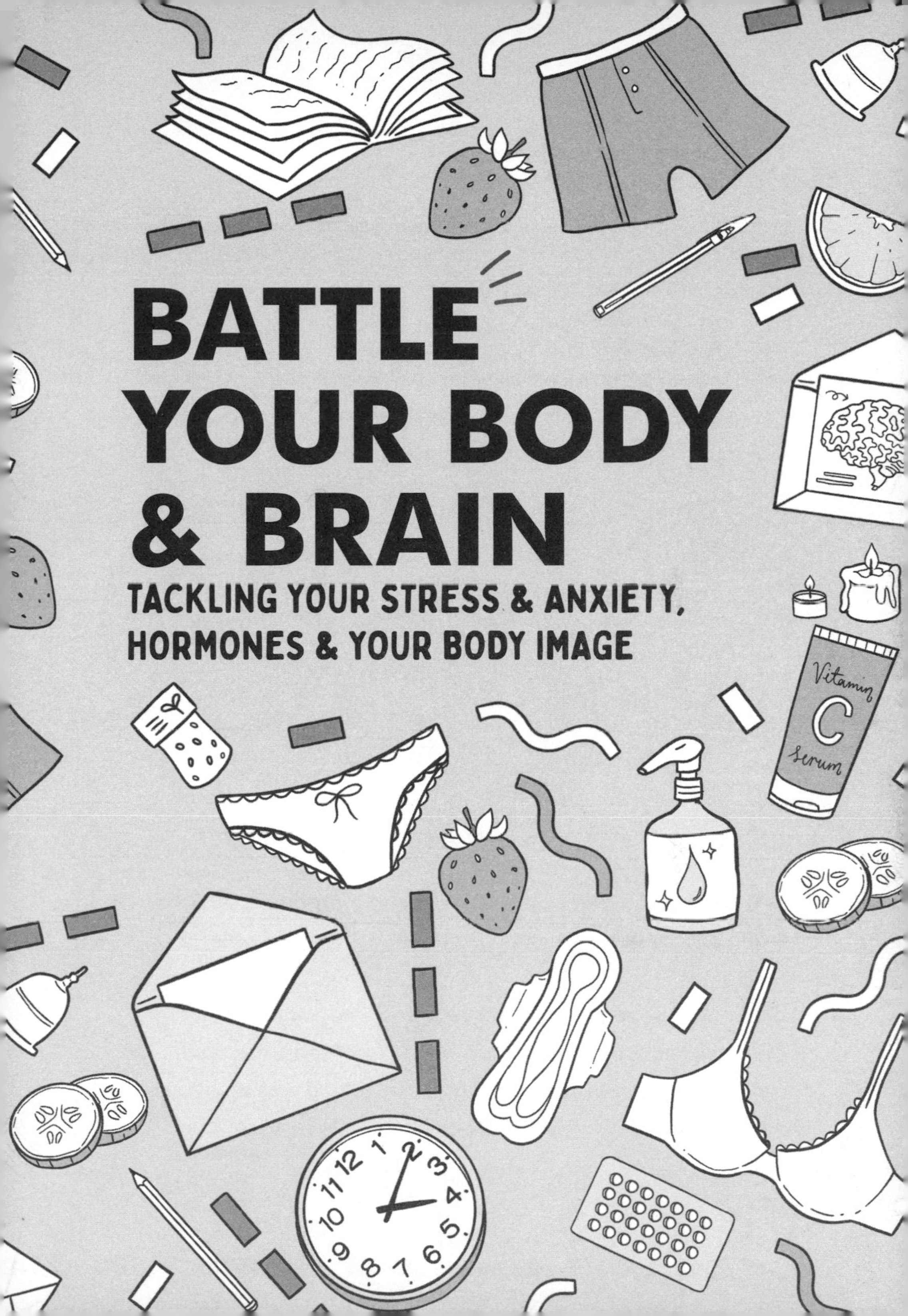
BATTLE YOUR BODY & BRAIN
TACKLING YOUR STRESS & ANXIETY, HORMONES & YOUR BODY IMAGE
Vitamin C serum

'Your body is your temple'

'Your body is your home'

Have you heard these Zen-like phrases? Well, sure. But there are times in our teenage years when it feels like our body's trying to steal some matches and burn the place down!

BUT. Our body carries us through life, so it's important for us to try and be friends with it, right?

Admittedly our bodies can be 'the difficult moody friend' at times. One day it might be a lovely fresh breakout of spots that have erupted on your chin, the next day you've ruined your only nice pair of pants because Mother Nature has decided to rock up unexpectedly, and by Friday you find yourself crying over a meme of a rescue kitten. Sure it's extreme, but it's totally normal, and it's all part of being a kick-ass young woman.

The ever-changing cycle of hormones that whiz around our bodies alter throughout the month, which can explain why we sometimes feel ... A LOT! But maybe we have a richer, more fulfilling experience in the world because of it? Even skincare brands are now putting out different skin products for each week of your cycle, so the world is catching on!

Sometimes I wish that, rather than having a period, I could just be sent a text like

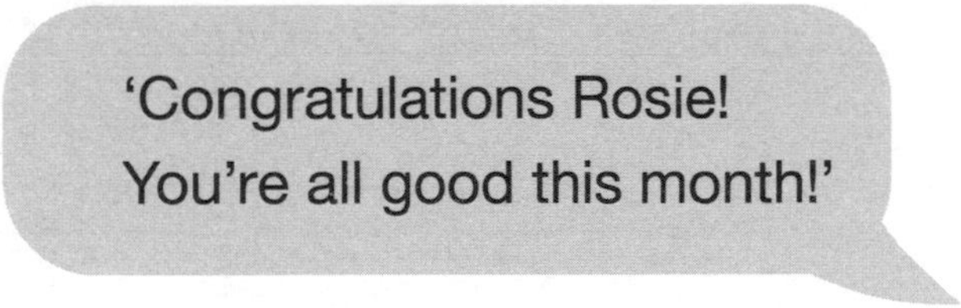

'Congratulations Rosie!
You're all good this month!'

... because having a period does mean your body is healthy and working as it should be. And bleeding for a week without dying surely must make us superhuman?

And then there's your beautiful brain because your mental health is just as important as your physical health. After all, if you break your leg, you're not expected to limp around untreated, and the same care should be taken for your mind, so do seek out help from mental health professionals if you need it.

Taking some time out to

is important. When I was younger, I was allowed to take what my mum called 'Rosie' Days (my name works on many levels!).

These were (what might nowadays be called 'Mental Health Days') days where I was just allowed to... *be*. To just exist. To unwind, to do things I loved, to unlearn and forget any bad things that might have been happening. Then the day after, I'd skip to school feeling much more capable of taking on the world!

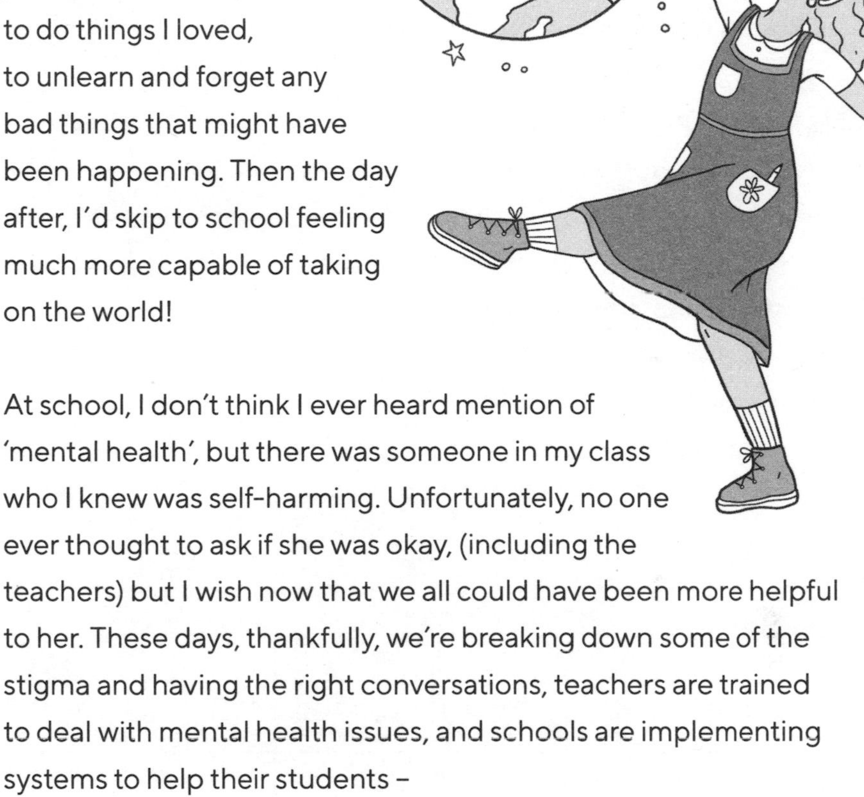

At school, I don't think I ever heard mention of 'mental health', but there was someone in my class who I knew was self-harming. Unfortunately, no one ever thought to ask if she was okay, (including the teachers) but I wish now that we all could have been more helpful to her. These days, thankfully, we're breaking down some of the stigma and having the right conversations, teachers are trained to deal with mental health issues, and schools are implementing systems to help their students –

so hopefully there is always someone you can turn to.

Because being a teenager can be hard. Our brains aren't fully developed until our mid-20s so no matter how brilliant you are at handling things, your brain is still growing like the rest of your body. It's no wonder you might sometimes feel 'You know what, I'm actually not ok!' And when that happens turn to people you know will listen: your GP, a friend or your family.

Depression, anxiety, stress, struggling with friends or your body image can all affect your mental health – and it is never anything to be ashamed of. Perhaps many of your favourite musicians, actors or celebrities have experienced these emotions too, so you're not alone in how you feel. If anything, it's something that unites us all as humans. I stress again, the most important thing with any kind of mental health issue, is to

If you suffer in silence, you might never get the help you need to overcome it.

In "Battle Your Body and Brain", we're going to cover the importance of putting yourself first, and looking after your mind and your body. I hope you come away with a sense of agency, with the knowledge that self-care really isn't selfish, but vital for your happiness and wellbeing and a crucial part of your armoury for

taking over the world!

> *"I'm an introverted extrovert. I have enough confidence to do stand-up comedy, but I don't have the confidence to wear a hat."*
>
> ROSE MATAFEO

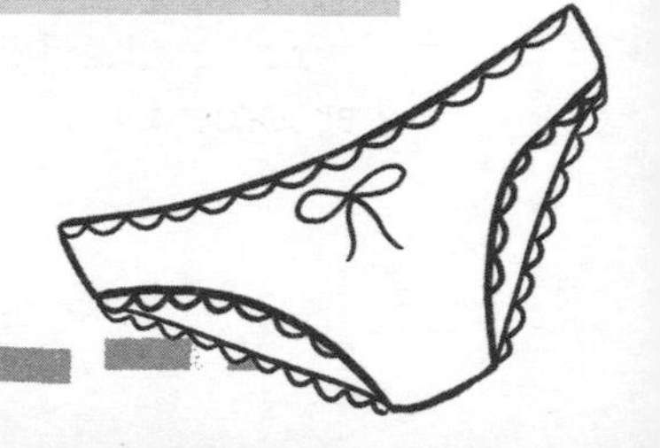

SKIN IN THE GAME, DR JUSTINE KLUK, CONSULTANT DERMATOLOGIST

When I was 12, I started to develop breakouts for the first time. It was only the occasional spot on my forehead to begin with, but then they started to increase in number, and spread to other parts of my face and body. Before long, it felt like there wasn't a single day that I didn't wake up without a new breakout somewhere.

To start with, there wasn't anyone in my group of friends who suffered with acne, and my parents didn't seem too concerned about it. My Dad told me he'd had acne in his teens and that I would grow out of it. So, I dabbled with various skincare products that were lying around at home, applied dabs of toothpaste and the like, and just hoped for the best. All the while, I felt more and more self-conscious about how I looked, and I remember spending hours in the bathroom before school or meeting up with friends trying to cover up my spots with concealer.

I grew up in South Africa and had lots of sun exposure as a young child. At some point my Mom took me to see a dermatologist to get a mole on my shoulder checked out. The first thing the doctor said when we entered the office was 'Never mind her mole. What are you doing about her acne?'

I remember feeling a mixture of horror and relief at the doctor's reaction. Horror – because obviously there was a real problem and this confirmed that it was noticeable to other people. And relief – because clearly it wasn't just in my head! Somebody was taking it seriously and wanted to help me. I was given medical treatment and skincare advice and my spots improved. Hurray!

I wish I could tell you that that's where the story ends and that I've never had a breakout since. But as many people with acne will find out, it can be more of a long-term condition for some of us and it can flare up again from time to time throughout life. Knowing that there is effective treatment available and that there are people you can turn to when it gets you down is both reassuring and empowering. It's also one of the main reasons I decided to become a dermatologist myself.

These days I get to help people just like the 'teenage me' in my clinic. Acne is visible and because it's so common, everyone thinks they're an expert. This means lots of people feel like they can comment on your skin. Sadly, it's not unusual to feel embarrassed, ashamed or self-conscious about how you look if you have acne. I have often thought about what I would have wanted to know at an early stage if I had my time again and I'd like to share with you a bit of skin science and a few pointers for managing breakouts ...

Firstly, what is acne and why does it happen?

Acne is the medical term used to describe breakouts. It affects approximately 85% of young adults between the ages of 12 to 25 years. This means that for many of us, our first experience of acne is during puberty when our bodies start to produce higher levels of hormones known as androgens. The best-known example is testosterone.

The oil-producing glands in our skin are very sensitive to changes in hormones and begin to step up the production of sebum, the natural oil produced by our skin, when testosterone levels rise. As well as causing the skin to look greasy and congested, this sebum mixes with dead skin cells and blocks our pores leading to blackheads, pus-filled spots and sometimes deeper pimples known as nodules or cysts.

Acne can also leave dark marks on the skin, known as post-inflammatory hyperpigmentation, or scarring, which can be raised or indented. Some of these marks can be permanent so treating acne effectively at an early stage is the best method of prevention.

There are a number of potential causes for acne and any combination of these could be acting at the same time.

1

Genes play an important role. Having a strong family history of acne and onset at an early age can lead to more severe or persistent cases.

2

Hormones can definitely cause acne to flare up, which is why many girls have increased breakouts around the time of their period.

3

Underlying medical conditions such as polycystic ovarian syndrome (PCOS) increase the risk of acne and may be tested for in girls if there are other symptoms to suggest it, for example, carrying extra weight, thinning of scalp hair, excess body hair and irregular periods. PCOS has been estimated to affect approximately 8% of females of reproductive age, making it very common indeed.

4

Lifestyle factors can also contribute. Stress, wearing certain types of make-up, using the wrong skincare products or even following very complex, multi-step skincare routines can play a role.

5

There is lots of speculation about the role of diet in acne and a lot we still need to learn. Foods with a high glycaemic index (think sugary and processed foods) have been shown to increase breakouts, and there is some evidence to suggest that dairy aggravates acne for some people.

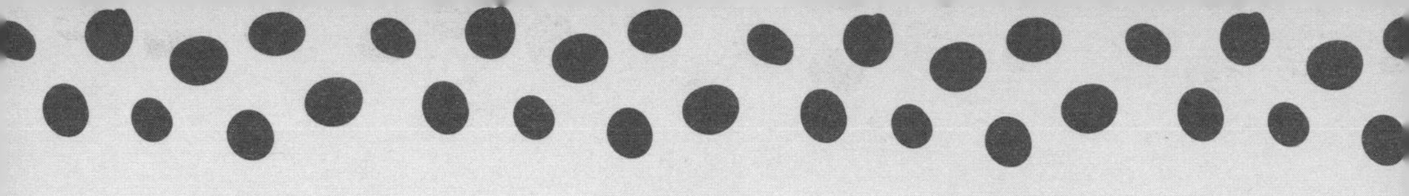

So what can we do to treat acne?

Establishing a good skincare routine is an important first step. Here are some things to consider when working out your routine:

1 Wash your face morning and evening with a mild cleanser. I like a gel or cream cleanser. For those with very oily skin, a foaming cleanser may help to reduce shine

2 Blackheads and acne don't occur because you are dirty, so scrubbing too hard or using harsh exfoliators, is not particularly helpful and may actually increase redness and swelling.

3 Apply a sun protection moisturiser or sunscreen after cleansing in the morning. Acne blemishes can leave dark marks on the skin if not properly protected from the UV rays in sunlight. Choose a broad spectrum product with SPF30 or 50. Broad spectrum means the sunscreen protects you from both UVA and UVB. Tinted sunscreens containing the ingredient iron oxides may be more effective for post-inflammatory hyperpigmentation. Always check the label for the words 'non-comedogenic', which means the product won't block the pores

4 There are some really good products for concealing acne blemishes and improving your self-confidence. Mineral make-up is especially great for absorbing excess oil. Green tinted creams are good for dialling down redness.

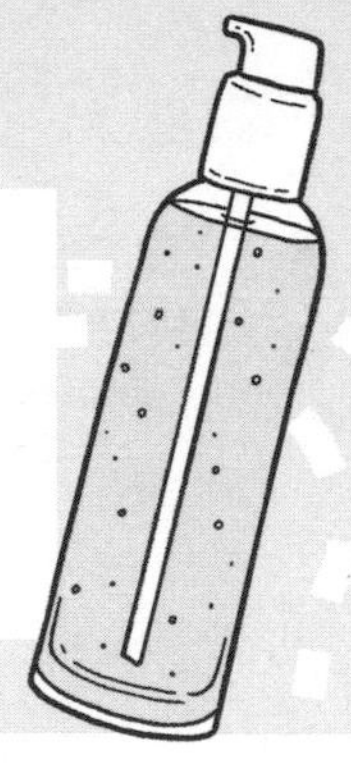

5 In the evenings, targeted acne-fighting products containing ingredients like benzoyl peroxide, zinc, sulphur, niacinamide, azelaic acid or salicylic acid can be applied to affected areas after cleansing. Be careful about combining lots of different active ingredients together as this can really irritate the skin. Start with one and see how you go.

6 Follow with a lightweight moisturiser. People who have breakouts often skip moisturiser, but moisturising makes it easier for your skin to handle active ingredients that may otherwise cause dryness and peeling. Again, make sure that moisturisers or any other leave-on products are labelled non-comedogenic.

7 Wash your hair regularly and tie it back away from your face. Greasy hair, or applications of hair serums and gels, can cause breakouts on the forehead, particularly along the hair line.

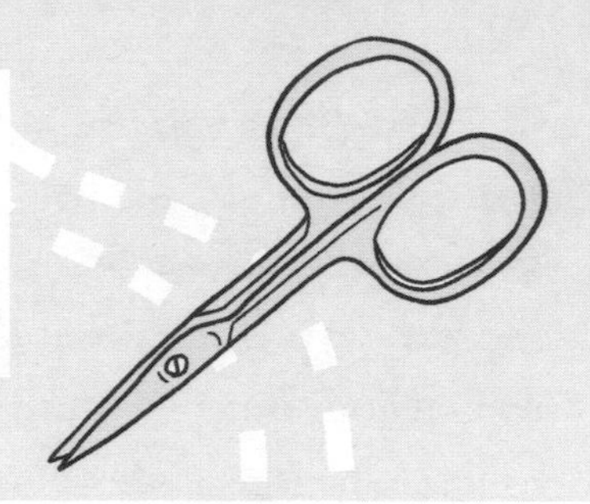

8 Remove sweaty clothes as soon as possible after sport or exercise and hop in the shower as promptly as you can.

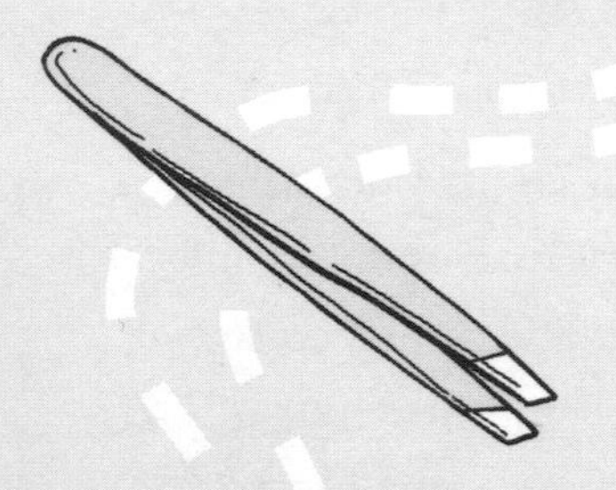

9 For anyone who shaves, be careful to avoid cutting or scraping any existing spots. Clean the blade regularly, make sure it is sharp and shave in the direction of the hair growth.

10 Try to break the habit of touching your face and, whatever you do, do not squeeze or pick your pimples. This can introduce infection and may also lead to permanent scarring.

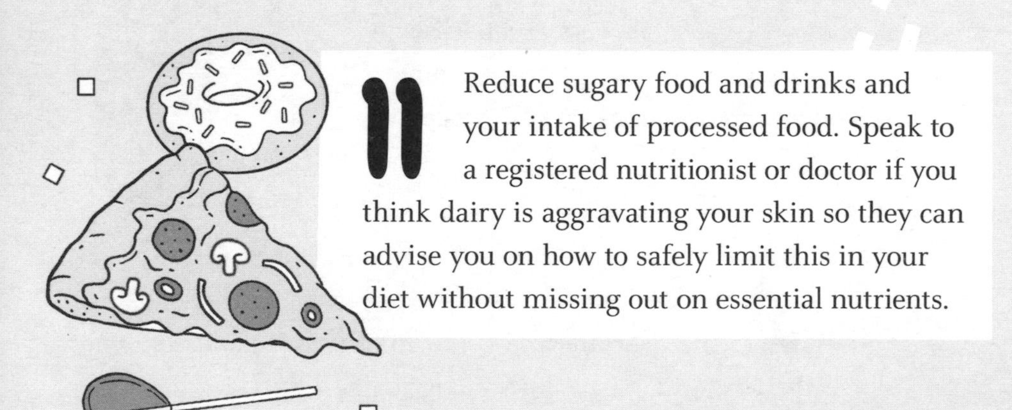

11 Reduce sugary food and drinks and your intake of processed food. Speak to a registered nutritionist or doctor if you think dairy is aggravating your skin so they can advise you on how to safely limit this in your diet without missing out on essential nutrients.

What should we do if the self-care techniques aren't working?

If you have multiple red and inflamed bumps, if you are developing dark marks or signs of scarring, or if acne is starting to impact your self-esteem, it is definitely worth taking steps to see your family doctor or dermatologist to get the condition under control. There are a range of effective treatment options.

So don't just sit back and wait for it to pass. There are people out there who can help.

Good luck!

SLAY YOUR FEARS & SELF-DOUBTS, DR JULIE SMITH, CLINICAL PSYCHOLOGIST

You won't remember this, but when you were a toddler, learning to walk, you'd have fallen over roughly 69 times every hour. That's a lot of failure! But at no point did you ever doubt that you could do it. At no point did you ever stop to think about giving up and just crawling everywhere instead. You just kept trying to walk

for the fun of it.

But, as we get older and the world starts telling us what we should do, how we should do it, and what we should look like while we're doing it, the voice of self-doubt starts to creep into your head.

It's an annoying little voice that wasn't there when you were learning to walk and regales you with comments like, 'You can't do it. Don't even try. Everyone will laugh. You're not clever enough, pretty enough, strong enough, tall enough, short enough

blah,

blah,

blah.'

Most people spend a lifetime battling with that voice of self-doubt in their heads. They try desperately to be *enough* – whatever the world is telling them enough is right now.

But here's the thing about that voice of self-doubt ... It has good intentions. It is trying to keep you safe. But if you let it make all your decisions, it just tells you to hide away, stay small, stay quiet, stay invisible. Then life stops being so fun.

Self-doubt also has a good friend called Fear. They often turn up together.

Fear is another feeling that's trying to keep you safe. But fear gets it wrong sometimes. Fear can tell you something is not possible when actually, it is. So, unless you are in real danger, don't let fear make your decisions for you. If something really matters to you, pack fear in your bag and bring it along for the ride. Frankly, a roller coaster without fear wouldn't be so exciting, would it?

When I was training to be a psychologist, I had to do a viva exam. It's the scariest kind of exam where you sit in front of a panel of experts and answer questions. I was filled with fear. Just before I went in, I saw another girl run out of the exam room in tears. I started to question if I could do this.

Then someone turned to me and gave me some of the best advice I've ever had.

Enjoy it.

he said.

This is your opportunity to show off all that you have been working on.

In that moment I experienced a massive shift from fear for excitement. This scary exam turned from a desperate attempt to avoid failure into a challenge that I could enjoy. My heart was still racing and my palms were still sweaty, but I remembered that the stress I felt was my body gearing me up to focus and perform at my best.

Shifting my perspective shifted the whole experience. From that moment on, I knew how to deal with my fear and the battle inside my head. I no longer focused only on avoiding failure. I focused on the enjoyment of doing my best – whatever the outcome. I still use it to this day. When I first got the opportunity to talk on the radio and the television, the fear and self-doubt could have consumed me and made me decide not to do it. But instead, I chose to enjoy it and that's exactly what I did.

So, when you face something that feels like
a threat and the fear rises up, ask yourself,

how can I see this as a CHALLENGE that I can get EXCITED about?

Instead of focusing on the outcome, focus instead on enjoying the process, getting curious and fascinated by new experiences and learning from everything whether it goes well or not.

One of the biggest fears of our teen years is what others think of us. Sometimes you want to fit in and sometimes you want to be different and that's normal. But as you discover more about the kind of person you want to be, you start to realise that there are only a few opinions that really matter.

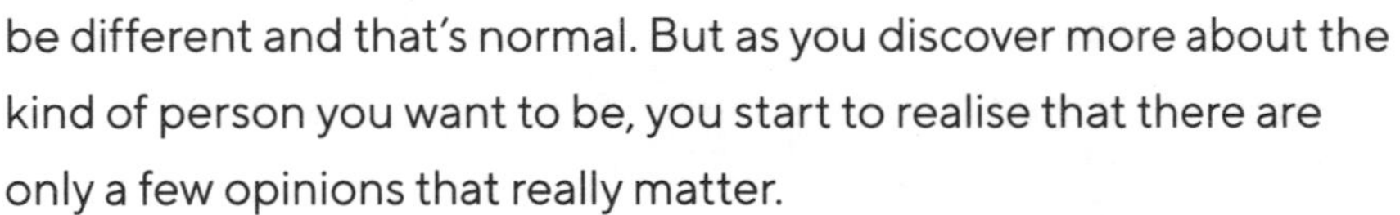

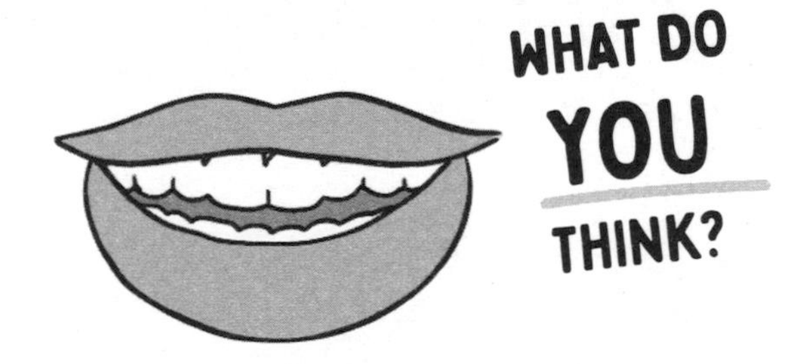

The opinions that matter most will be the people you respect the most and who love you unconditionally. The most important person to get approval from, is you. It's ok to flex and turn and try out new identities and experiences. But in the end,confidence comes from knowing that you are enough as you are.

You can learn, try new things, strive to be the best version of you, and feel the fear along the way. But whatever happens, you are still you, and that is enough.

Whatever is going on in your life as you read this, I know you will understand what it means to feel pain and sadness. Growing up is hard and it's normal for it to be full of ups and downs.

Sometimes you feel like you just want someone to tell you what to do. I'm not going to tell you what to do. Because, as it turns out, every struggle that you face, you will find a way through it. And each time you do, it helps you to become the brilliant person you are going to be.

When times are tough and you are battling with loneliness, sadness, confusion or any other painful feeling, there is just one thing to remember. You have strength inside you that you haven't even tapped into yet. Each time you face something tough and you don't know what to do, you discover a little more of that strength.

And every time you do that,

your confidence

grows

a little more ...

A LETTER TO TEENAGE ME, TANYA BURR, ACTOR & INFLUENCER

Hi Teenage Me,

I'm in my early 30s now and I don't know if you're going to find this encouraging or scary, but, I am still figuring out this thing we call Life. However, I have learnt a lot since I was your age and I do have some thoughts to share with you.

Your early teenage years will be some of the hardest of your life. You will experience depression for the first time, but not even be able to identify the scary thoughts in your head as that. I wish more than anything that I could give you a hug in this time and assure you: you will get through this! The most important thing I need you to know is that you are not alone.

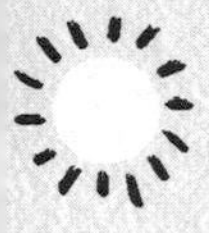

No matter what thoughts you're having, they are okay; people all over the world experience overwhelming thoughts and feelings every day. I know it feels terrifying and you think there's something wrong with you, so you choose to refuse any help in an effort to avoid confronting your feelings, but this will only make it worse. When you start to be more curious about how you think instead of simply being afraid, you'll be able to work through what's going on in your head and you'll discover some incredible coping mechanisms for those dark days.

BATTLE GEAR FOR DARKER DAYS

Please remember also, that your

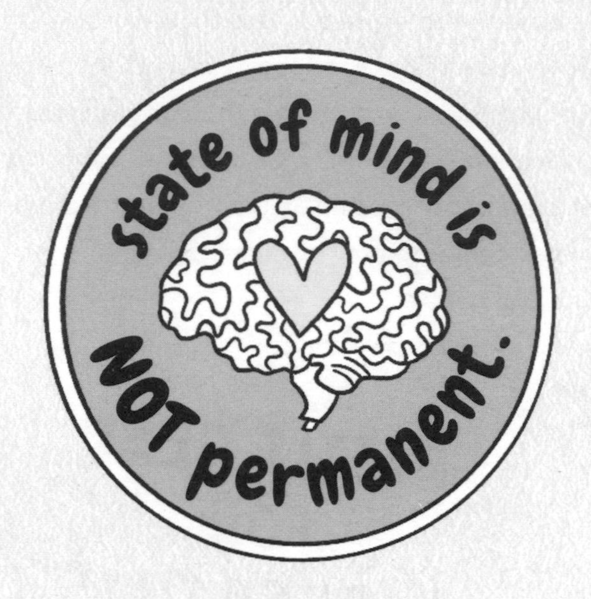

Anxiety and depression will come in waves throughout your life, but I promise you it gets better.

Don't be ashamed of your thoughts. I know 'mental health' isn't something you feel comfortable discussing and that's probably because people don't speak about it as much as they do now, but please understand, teenage me, that it's just as important as your physical health and really is something that needs all your care and attention. The same way as you care about not catching a cold and eating a vegetable every now and then, you can care about talking to someone about how you're feeling and finding ways to make your head a happier place.

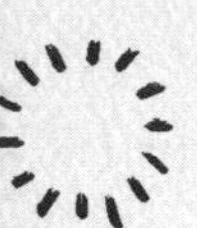

I know better than anyone (of course!) how important control is to you. The world seems like a scary place for you right now and you feel that controlling everything will keep you safe, but what you don't realise is that you're carrying the weight of the world on your shoulders ... and that is exhausting. By relinquishing some of this control and allowing yourself to trust that things will be okay, you will gain so much mental freedom!

Now, we need to have a little conversation about your mid- to late teens. On a positive note, your mental health will be in a much more manageable place, with anxiety coming and going, rather than consuming you every day. However, on a less positive note, you're going to make some questionable choices. Part of me wants to say 'go for it' and *not* give you any advice here, as you've made some pretty hilarious memories for me. I have literally THE BEST evenings reminiscing with the girls about the infamous mullet haircuts and how we practically competed for how many different boys we could kiss in one night.

Talking of the girls, hold them close, the same ones that you're getting into trouble with now are the ones that are going to stick with you for life. Don't always take their advice though: your MSN name does NOT define who you are as a person and drinking neat vodka is NEVER a good idea.

I hope this has given you a little comfort. Remember, you have a loving family, amazing friends and you have so much going for you. Most of all, you are safe. I feel like you really need to hear that. You're going to have a truly special and amazing life, nothing is the way you think it will be, but believe me when I say this ... it's so much better.

KATIE PI. ER
'VISIBLY DIFFERENT' ICON

'Even when you think things can never move forward and you feel so low, there's always a way out.'

If there's one truth in life, it's that we cannot control what happens to us, but we can control how we react. And Katie Piper is perhaps the embodiment of this mantra ...

In 2008, Katie was working towards achieving her dream of being on screen, working in TV presenting and modelling when an ex-lover conspired to commit an horrific acid attack on her. Katie's face was severely burnt due to the sulphuric acid used in the devastating assault. She lost vision in one eye and has since undergone multiple skin graft surgeries, and fortunately, an operation to restore her sight.

Katie bravely waived her right to anonymity in order to raise awareness for burns victims and in 2009, while still in the very early stages of her recovery Katie set up the Katie Piper Foundation. Her aim to promote the idea that being 'visibly different' should not limit someone's function, social inclusion or sense of well-being.

In 2018 the Foundation opened the UK's first residential burns rehab clinic. Katie has gone on to author several best-selling, confidence-building books and she has been involved in successful TV series and worked with amazing brands. Katie Piper continues to show the world that, with resilience and determination, you can overcome any obstacle life puts in front of you.

IT'S NOT YOUR JOB TO FIT CLOTHES; CLOTHES SHOULD FIT YOU, NAOISE DOLAN, AUTHOR

It started with a skirt.

I'm vegan so I don't buy animal fabrics new, but I see no issue with doing so secondhand. For a long time I'd dreamed of finding a leather pencil skirt in a vintage shop. I wanted it to sit just below my waist, the leather had to be supple, and the lining needed to be durable enough for easy care, yet breathable enough for hot days. It should have a covered zip and strong stitches. I became obsessed with these things as a teenager, and felt savvier and more equipped ever afterwards in shops. I take picky pleasure in pondering that I'm not paying that much for a poly blend that will fall apart in three washes, or for buttons that feel like they'd snap if I bit them.

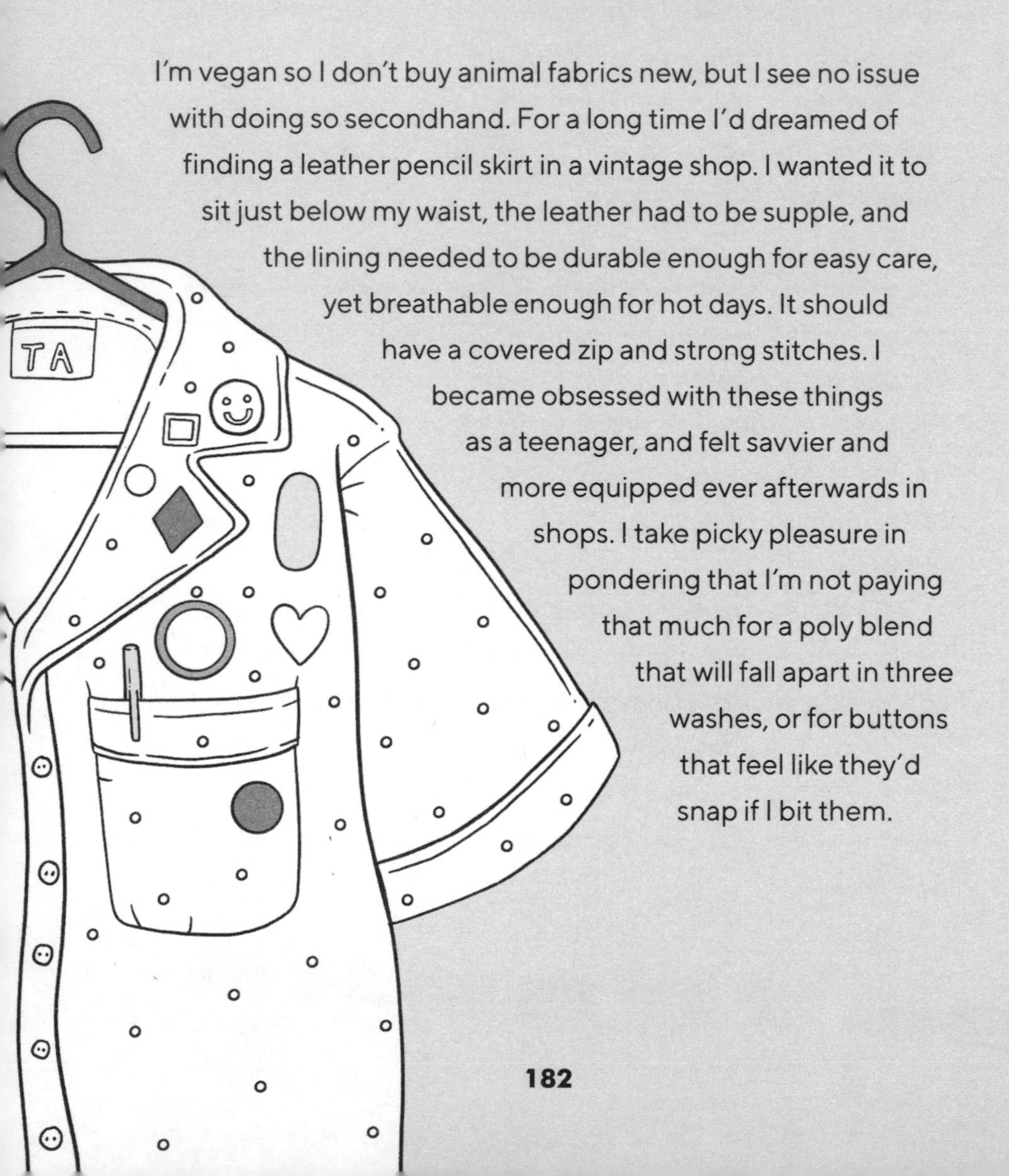

(I have never yet actually tested this with my teeth: I'd be banned from shops, and probably from life.)

I had no pressing need of the above article. 'There's no such thing as an urgent text', they say, and there's certainly no such thing as an urgent leather skirt. I was happy biding my time, knowing it might take years until I chanced on one that fit me perfectly and was well-made, at a price that didn't require me to pawn my kidneys.

And there it was.

I'd wandered into a vintage shop in North London with a view to finding a light summer dress. When I'm trawling through secondhand clothes I don't use my eyes – I run my fingers along the clothes rail. Fabric is the one thing you can never change, so it's the first thing you need to love. If I don't like touching something then I don't need to see it because I already know I'll hate wearing it.

My fingertips scanned for linen and cotton, but I landed on something else. It was the soft leather I'd wanted, and it was black.

I primed myself for disappointment as I took it the hanger from rack. The skirt would have some statement detail that I hated. I examined it: no maroon feathers, no puce contrast stitching. Fine, but it wouldn't be in my size. I held it against me: waist fine, hips fine. The lining would be a dense polyester that would have me

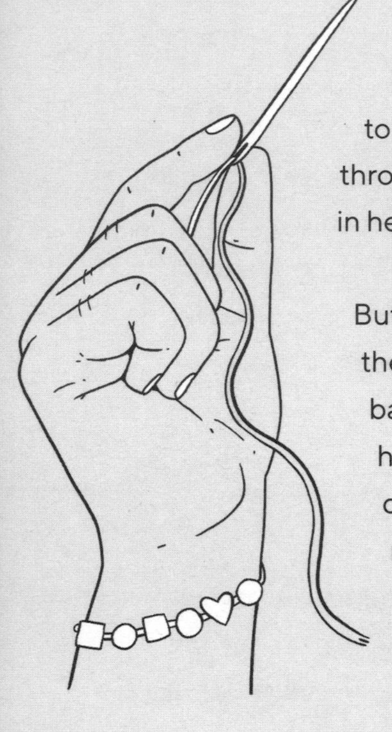

sweating till winter. I held the inner fabric up to the window and pinpricks of light showed through the weave – so it would let air circulate in heatwaves.

But in the changing room it cut off right at the knee, a length I hate on me. I started bargaining with myself. Maybe I could hold it up with a belt – though that would contravene my just-below-the-waist requirement. Maybe I could get the sewing kit out – I raise hemlines myself on simpler fabrics all the time, but I was nervous of trying it on leather. Maybe I could live with the length since all other boxes were ticked. What right did I have to be so fussy?

Then, when I chatted to the owner at the till, saying I loved the skirt but the length was wrong, she said:

'You could just get it taken up'.

I'd heard that a million times before in shops. Usually I'd dismissed it as sales patter. But it was a warm sunny day, she didn't seem pushy, and somehow it finally struck me that this was something I could do.

After I bought the skirt, it took a week before I mustered the courage to visit the tailor. When I was a teenager you could name any body part and I could tell you something I hated about mine, even the ones I didn't have. It was daunting to imagine a level of peace and comfort in myself where I could pay to have something look like it was made for me. In my bedroom I wore the skirt and measured until I knew exactly what I'd request: I wanted to avoid trying it on in front of the tailor.

The shop was filled with fabric rolls and recent orders hanging in wait to be collected.

'Could I have three inches off the hemline?' I said.

'Three inches?' the tailor said. 'Wow.'

'I'm short', I said.

The following week I collected my covered hanger, and prepared myself for disappointment all the way home, just as I'd done before trying on the skirt in the shop. But it was perfect.

This is what I want to tell my teenage self: it is not your job to fit clothes. Clothes should fit you. You're not too short; the skirt is too long.

If you look at the stiletto heels on celebrities and catwalk models, you'll see telltale signs that most are either too long or too wide for the wearer. You'll see the beginnings of hammer toes and bunions on women still in their twenties from over a decade of forcing their feet into those shoes.

This problem is less obvious with clothes because some styles are unfitted and all can be altered, but there is no sample-sized human being. All of us veer in some way from mass-produced measurements. Nearly everything is too long for me and it's either too loose on the waist or too tight on the hip. I'd always felt that was somehow my fault, and if I kept wearing things off the rack then eventually I'd find something that affirmed me as the standard woman.

I'm not her. I'm me. And while I don't have the time or budget to get everything altered, even knowing that I can has made a difference. Now, when I wear something that doesn't quite fit right, I don't think that's my problem. I think:

I'm perfect, and this dress would be too if I let my tailor at it.

YOUR MENTAL HEALTH MATTERS, DR NIHARA KRAUSE, CONSULTANT CLINICAL PSYCHOLOGIST & FOUNDER AND CEO, STEM4

> *"Adolescence is when the very worst and best impulses in the human soul struggle against each other for possession."*
>
> G. STANLEY HALL, 1846.

Adolescence is a formative stage, with unique physical, neurological, emotional, cognitive, behavioural and social changes that all collide. Unsurprisingly, adolescence is a psychologically vulnerable time, especially if impacted by changes including family dynamics and experiences, friendship and educational challenges and exposure to difficult experiences. Increased access to technology, particularly social media, has its own negatives, and creates a lack of censorship to age-appropriate information. This can promote a fast spread of triggering information, increasing negative emotions through comparison, as well as making it harder to separate real life from virtual – a negative at a time when, as a teenager, you are forming your identity.

Teenage mental ill health has finally become an area of important focus. With around

20% of adolescents globally experiencing a range of mental health difficulties, estimated to rise to

40% following the pandemic,

many would say this focus has come too late. It has been further highlighted by a quarter of adults also experiencing mental ill health. A lack of mental health resources for both adolescents and adults in the UK, at primary care and specialist level, make things look further dismal.

However, there is a huge amount that can be done to bring about positive change, and since 2011, this has been the impetus of stem4, a leading teenage mental health charity of which I am founder.

Here are some tips on the areas that need our focus:

The **promotion** of mental health awareness and **prevention** of mental ill health is essential, challenging the stigma around it, as well as educating on early signs and symptoms and steps to change.

Promoting and building positive mental health through healthy sleep and eating patterns, establishing a regular activity schedule, learning good social and interpersonal skills, engaging with our community, developing a positive sense of self, learning to problem solve, and identifying and regulating emotions are all helpful resilience factors outlined in my MINDYOUR5 model which can be seen on stem4's website.

These kind of 'prevention interventions' aim to strengthen a young person's ability to reduce risk-taking behaviours as well as promote building self-worth, self-esteem and self-acceptance. Building family resilience include establishing sound parenting skills, developing good quality family relationships and positive parental mental health.

Individuality needs to be addressed since no one person or group will experience mental health difficulties similarly, nor are the causes the same. The unique experiences and characteristics that underlie the condition needs to be acknowledged and tailored help offered to each person.

Early intervention is crucial since this leads to better outcomes. Learning the early signs of an emerging mental ill health condition and what effective, evidence-based treatment are available will help. As a result, intervention needs to have a multi-level approach provided through a range of methods including:

traditional talking treatments (like Cognitive Behavioural Therapy or CBT)

digital approaches (such as online resources such as the stem4 mental health apps and website)

peer-to-peer trained support

parent and family approaches

access to medical or pharmaceutical support where needed.

Easy to access expert and specialist resources for moderate to severe mental ill health conditions needs to be prioritised at a governmental level. stem4 will continue to deliver on all these points to enhance and enable young people's mental health to flourish.

You can visit our website for more information and resources on anxiety, depression, eating disorders and more.

Alternatively, you can download our one-of-a-kind apps that will help you manage your anxiety, low moods or depression and help friends and families to provide mental health support.

PERIODS & YOU, GABBY EDLIN, CEO OF BLOODY GOOD PERIOD

Hello lovely reader,

I'm here to talk to you about periods. Why? Well, in 2016 I started a period charity in the UK called **Bloody Good Period**. Its aim is to get period products to people who can't afford them, and the right medical education to people who don't have access to it.

But we also exist to NORMALISE periods, because even though they are well, *bloody normal,* you'd be forgiven for feeling shame or embarrassment, as there's still such a taboo around them. So, as you can imagine, I spend a lot of time talking about menstruation (the technical term for periods).

I thought I'd start by telling you about my first period. You're maybe around the age you'll be expecting yours, or perhaps you've already started and are just feeling nosy or have lots of questions. I've got you, pal. I also think it's really interesting to hear about other people's first periods. It can tell you a lot about how comfortable they are with menstruation and their bodies in general.

We don't have enough (or even good!) period education in the UK so it's really not your fault if you're like ...

errr ... what the hell is going on here?

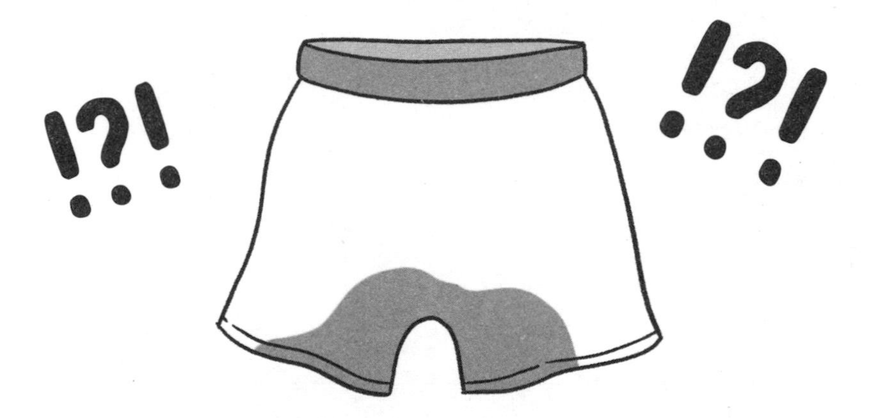

There isn't enough room here to tell you everything, but I have recommended some good books below. Also, you really should get this education in school. If you're not, I'd recommend petitioning your teachers to introduce it!

But back to my bloody story ...

My first period happened on a Saturday morning when I was around 13 years old. I had eaten three Cadbury's creme eggs the night before. No reason why, I just really like them. But I didn't normally eat three, and I got a tummy ache. However, it was a different tummy ache to the creme egg kind (You know what I mean ...) and it turns out that's because it was my very first period pain (Yay ...)

Other than that it was pretty uneventful. I knew what to expect because I was the last of my friends to start, and so everyone talked about it all the time.

However, no one situation is the same, so if you've already started your period, or you haven't yet, or you don't anticipate that you ever will (perhaps you were assigned male at birth but want to support your menstruating friends). I've put together some facts for you. Most of these I certainly didn't know when I was a teenager, but I would have certainly benefitted from knowing them all.

I won't tell you the technical stuff you can learn in biology, and this is by no means an exhaustive list. You can grab quite a few brilliant books from the library that will tell you more. My absolute favourite is *Period* by Natalie Byrne and you should also check out *Red Moon Gang* by Tara Costello.

1 **Menstruating** (getting your period; bleeding from your vagina) does not make you an adult, and has absolutely no effect on whether you should (or can be, legally) sexually active. It is simply a stage in a girl or person with a womb's life that means their body is changing and preparing their reproductive organs, so that they're ready in the event that they want to have children later on.

2 **Your period** may not be regular for quite some time. In fact, it can take years to become regular. You can work this out by tracking your period (i.e. the when you actually bleed) as well as other things (e.g. feeling down, feeling more energetic and so on)..

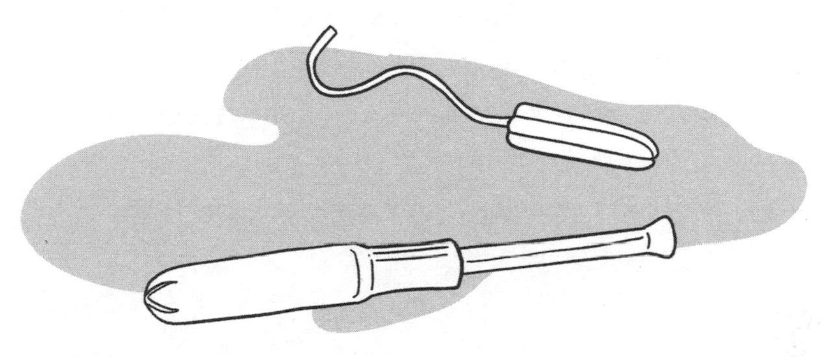

3 **Tracking your period** and, in fact, **your whole cycle** is incredibly helpful. You can do this on your smartphone, or even better in a paper diary or notebook. Keep a note of how you feel on each day – your mood, your body, your energy levels – and when you have your period, whether it's heavy (i.e. are you changing your pad or tampon more often than once an hour?) You might start to notice patterns that will help you anticipate how you feel, and so you will be able to prepare for that.

4 If you have any questions at all, **ask your GP**. You can absolutely request that you have a female doctor, but remember that half the population menstruates so it's more than likely a male doctor has heard it all before.

5 If you've reached out to your GP and they just don't seem to get it, or you feel they aren't listening to you, ask to see another. This is completely valid. Keep going until you get the answers you deserve!

6 **There's more to life than tampons and pads.** If you're interested in eco-friendly options, you could try a **menstrual cup**; they take some time to get used to but some people love them! Or **period pants** – underwear specifically made

to hold a few tampons worth of blood without leaking. Clever huh?! There are also reusable pads which some people love because they're much more comfortable than disposable pads. All you have to do is chuck them in the wash after using. However, absolutely no judgement on the products you choose. It's your body, you know it best

7 And by the way, **periods are not dirty**. They're sometimes messy if you leak, or you get blood on your fingers, and of course you have to wash anything with blood on it, but really, as much as society and misinformed people might tell you, period blood is no more dirty and no more 'gross' than blood that comes from cutting your finger.

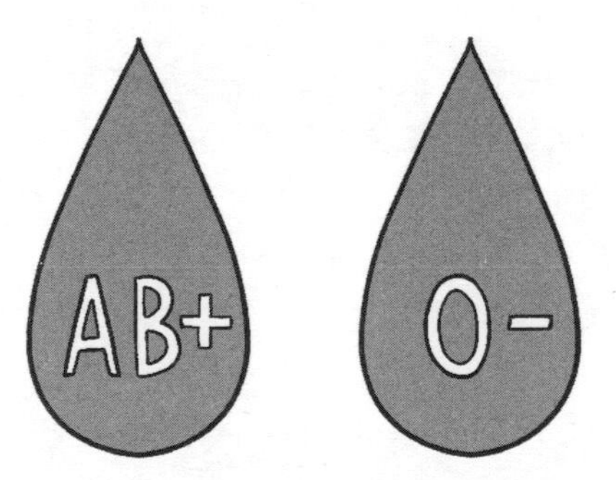

8 And **periods are nothing to be ashamed of**. They are a very normal part of life for half of the population. We're in a weird place in society where loads of people are still influenced by adverts, their parents, teachers, old books and films and think that periods should be shameful and never talked about. And then there's the rest of us who know that this is all a dirty trick

to try and keep women down (although not all people who bleed are women, and not all women bleed!) and we have nothing to be ashamed of. Imagine this as a spectrum and have a think about where you are on that spectrum, and what kind of conversations and musings you can have to meet us at that #NOSHAMEHERE point! P.S. We are ALL learning and you should never feel ashamed of being ashamed!

9 If you struggle to afford products and you're at school or in education, ask a trusted teacher if they are signed up with the UK Government Scheme to get free products for your school or college.

10 If you want to find out more about the politics of periods – you know, campaigning, normalising and even period poverty, just head to our website (see Resources on page 340) or find us on social media!

See you there – and wishing you a

BLOODY GOOD PERIOD!

10 TOP TIPS FOR MINDFULNESS

1 OHMMMMM

Why not try some mindful meditation? As someone who finds it impossible to sit still and finds anything like this slightly humorous, I really didn't know where to start. Meditation is an ancient art that has been practiced for centuries and involves sitting quietly, focusing on your breathing, your thoughts, the sensations in your body and the things you can hear around you. If, like me, you find it hard to do this yourself, the best place to start is a meditation app or a guided meditation online.

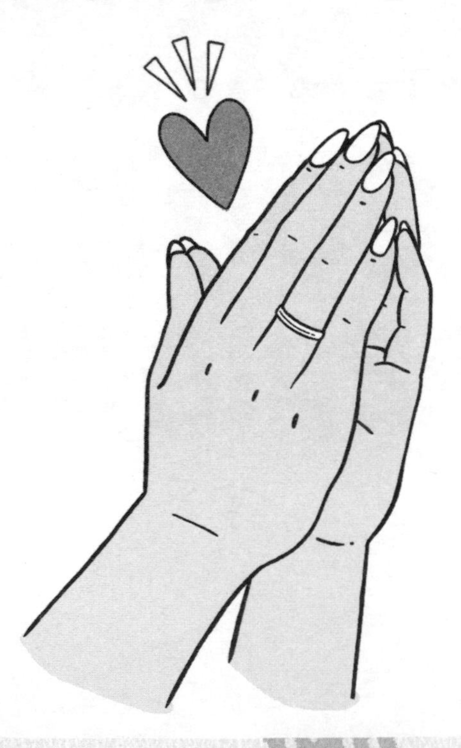

2 BREATHE IT OUT

Breathing techniques are generally used in meditation but you can also practise them at other times to combat stress or anxiety or just to calm you. Try the 4-7-8 technique, where you inhale through your nose for four seconds, hold your breath for seven seconds, and then slowly breathe out through your mouth for eight seconds, repeat as needed until you feel calmer. I love this technique – it works like a miracle before going on stage!

3 TAKE A DIP

Baths! I cannot stress enough the importance of submerging yourself in warm water to relax and unwind and bring a bit of mindfulness back into your life. Or, if you don't have access to a bath, take a long hot shower. Taking a bath half an hour before going to bed improves your sleep and adding essential oils or magnesium salts can relax and revive your muscles and rid your body of any unwanted tension.

MINDFUL EATING 4

I know that sounds strange, why do we need to focus mindfully on something we've done all our lives? But so often I spend half an hour making a nice meal and it's gone in under five minutes. Try eating slowly, focus on the delicious flavours and on chewing each mouthful properly, taking your time to enjoy it. Mindful eating not only aids your digestion but makes eating your breakfast/ lunch/dinner so much more enjoyable!

5 PUT THE DAMN PHONE DOWN

Keep phone and computer time within limits. Of course, this makes me sound like a parent, but the blue light your devices emit not only can give you eye strain, but can also stop you from accessing the good deep sleep we all need to function. It takes a huge amount of willpower to put these devices down (and leave them there) as we are all addicted to the dopamine hit we get from them. But try to limit your phone use and it will benefit your mental health!

6 FOCUS, FOCUS, FOCUS

The more we multi-task the more we make room for mistakes. So make a list of things you need to do, and approach them one task at a time, and don't start a new one until you've finished the last. I always have about five projects on the go at one time and trying to do too many things at once makes it a nightmare to finish any of them. So approaching things mindfully and methodically is the best thing to do.

TAKE TIME TO LISTEN 7

Often, I can be in a conversation and, without realising it, I've totally zoned out and can't tell you anything that was said in the last five minutes. If this sounds familiar to you, then it might be good to try listening mindfully ... If you enjoy listening to music, whack up the volume on a song you've never listened to before. Concentrate on all the different sounds you can hear: the instrumental, the bass, the lyrics. Really try and listen in a conscious and mindful way, while not trying to do anything else at the same time.

8 JUMP TO IT

The idea of 'active relaxation' might seem somewhat counter-intuitive but when we exercise our bodies release chemicals called endorphins that make us feel good – plus, exercise is a wonderful distraction if you've got something worrying you or playing on our mind. But it needn't be running or hitting the exercise bike, I find that yoga, stretching or gentle online exercise tutorials can mellow me right out at the end of a busy week.

WRITE IT DOWN 9

Journalling is a great way to make sense of your thoughts by getting them out of your head and down on to the page. Five minutes a day to write down what you're thinking helps make your feelings feel more manageable. Some people journal in the morning as soon as they wake up so they can start the day afresh and set goals for the day, and others prefer last thing before bed so they can have a peaceful night's rest. Keep a pen and notepad by your bed and see if this works for you.

10 BE A NATURE LOVER

Being outside in nature will help you create a more mindful state. Being among trees, in forests and woods, or by lakes, rivers and streams genuinely lifts my mood into a state of peace and mindfulness. To think, I used to be in a grump when I was made to walk the dog on a Sunday afternoon, but I would always come back feeling so much lighter. Fresh air has some magic (scientific) powers – and always lifts your mood.

STEP 4
WORLD
PEACE

PREPARE FOR THE ARMAGEDDON

TALKING ABOUT CONSENT, STANDING UP FOR WHAT YOU BELIEVE IN AND FINDING YOUR OWN BRAND AND STYLE

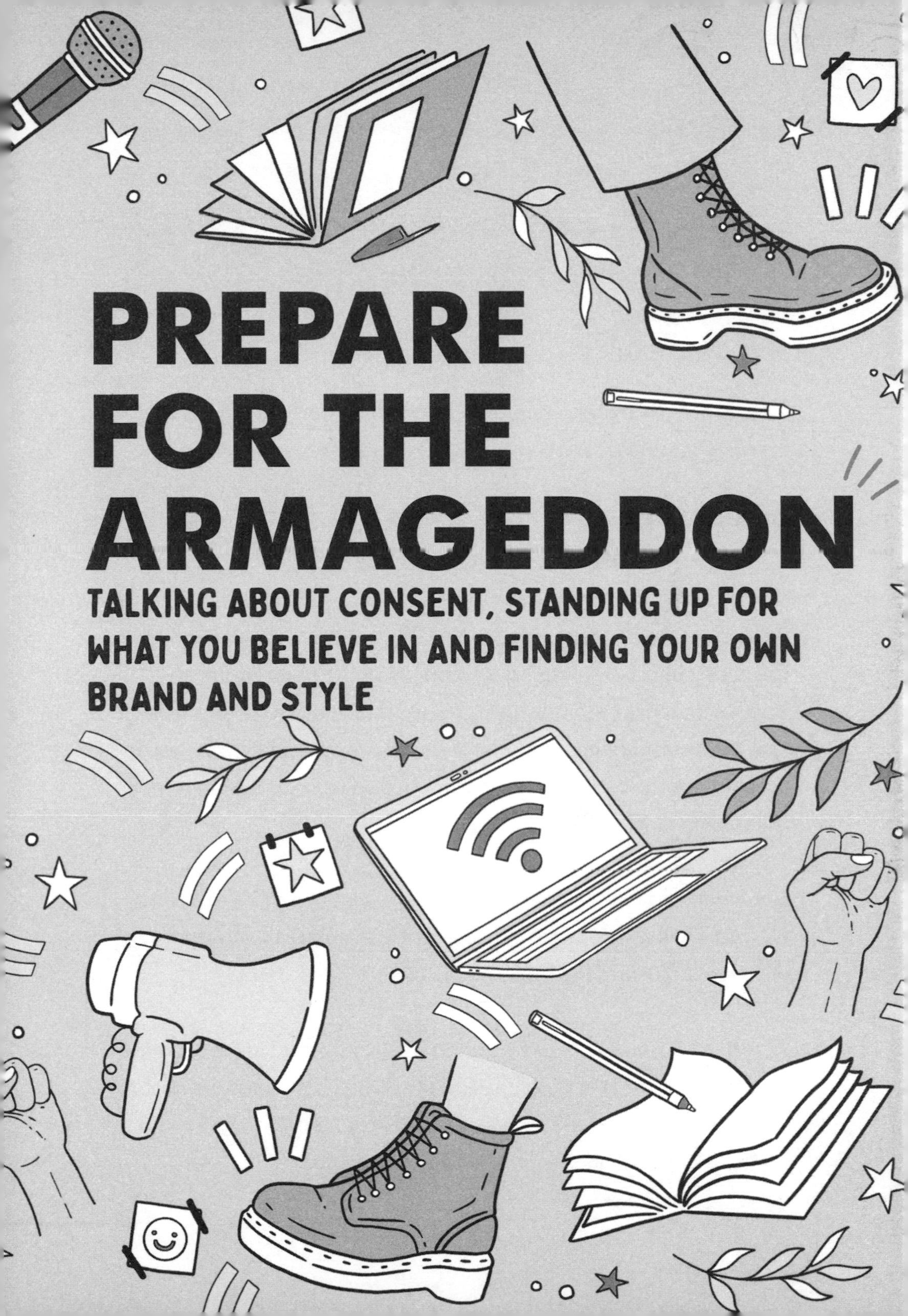

> *"Why can't I try on different lives, like dresses, to see which fits best and is more becoming?"*
>
> SYLVIA PLATH

This quote is from the writer and feminist Sylvia Plath and, in my opinion, touches on how often we change as young women.

Who am I?
Who do I want to be?

These were two questions I used to think about a lot. At sixth form, I accidentally enrolled on a philosophy course. Sure, it encouraged me to think about my existence, but it meant that I spent a week crying into my coffee with the idea that I was just a brain in a jar, and that life was something my mind had imagined to keep me entertained.

But what I did know is that I was someone who wanted to at least try and make a difference in the world. Because as young women, we have the power to shake things up and make change.

Just think about it ... *One Direction* were propelled to global fame due to the dedication and passion of young girls across the globe; Olivia Rodrigo's *Drivers License* had almost 39 million hits in the first week from teenage girls relating to it so hard ...

And the same can be said for ACTIVISM.

Incredible young women across the planet are fighting to get laws changed, motions passed, and are raising awareness of important issues like never before. Young women like Greta Thunberg and Malala Yousafzai are among the most well known, but there are many, many more!

Part of staging an Armageddon is getting out there and throwing your voice behind causes you are passionate about. So whether you're about to whack a megaphone on your Christmas list, get creative with protest placards or sign up to an online campaign, these things are all kick-ass steps in the process of making the world a better place!

In this section we're going to hear from amazing women who advocate for a plethora of hugely important subjects, such as how we tackle racism in today's society. Challenging, reporting, talking about and understanding racism are ways that we can help combat it. Supporting those who experience it, consciously lending our voices, time and resources to fight against it and being active bystanders, are key strategies in our battle for a fairer world!

In this section we also discuss why we need to take care of the planet. Because we can't take over the world if there isn't a world to take over ... Human beings have caused huge damage, but it's not too late to make a change. That might be stopping the harvesting of the rainforest, saving bees (Did you know that without bees our plants would not be pollenated, and we'd eventually run out of food?) or switching to cleaner energy. We can save the planet if we all come together now to try and help it.

We also discuss the importance of consent. As young woman, it's important to realise the power of the word 'No'; that we don't have to please others all the time, and we are always within our rights to turn something down – be that a date, a shoulder massage or a meet-up with friends. 'No' is a full sentence, and we don't need to spend time explaining our reasons behind it, even if people make us feel otherwise.

When our love interests start to develop, it can sometimes be confusing. But love is love, and as Jóhanna Sigurðardóttir, the first openly gay Prime Minister of Iceland once said,

'It is absolutely imperative that every human being's freedom and human rights are respected, all over the world.'

And that includes who we love, so we discuss in this section supporting the LGBTQ+A community, because this Armageddon we're staging is inclusive of everyone.

As young women, we sometimes have to shout a little louder to be heard, but I truly believe teenage girls have the power to change the world. It may feel like a hard task at times, but whichever causes you support, I know you'll do it with passion and dedication and with the aim of changing our world for the better!

> *"The way I dress and carry myself, a lot of people find it intimidating. I think my whole career can be boiled down to one word I always say in meetings: STRENGTH."*
>
> LORDE

YOU ARE NOT YOUR HAIR,
TỌLÁ OKOGWU, AUTHOR & HAIR CARE EDUCATOR

Dear teenage Tọlá,

No, you didn't go through with your silly threat to shorten your name to Jo and yeah, you're spelling your name with the accents now. Bet you're wondering why I'm writing to you though, huh? Well, I came back in literary time to tell you one simple truth. Wait for it...

You are not your hair!

You're probably thinking – why is she yapping on about hair instead of giving me winning lottery numbers or the answers to my looming exams? Well in a way, your hair will become your very own lottery ticket. Besides, it's not your exams you have to worry about. Quick tip to self: don't do that A level in Computing ... just don't.

Anyway back to your hair. You already know by now that Afro hair isn't just hair. It hasn't been for a very long time. It symbolises so much history and pain for Black people. Society has judged you by it, so-called 'friends' have ridiculed you for it, and you still tie yourself up in knots just trying to understand it. Right now, you're grappling to make sense of this strange inheritance, when all you really want is to have Laura from 9G's silky straight, blonde mane.

Yes, I know it's totally not fair and as you navigate it all, I'm going to need you to remember that ....

You are not your hair.

Sure, it's a part of you, but it is not ALL of you. It is not a measure of your worth or your beauty, no matter what those stupid magazines try and tell you. (You really need to stop reading those by the way.) *Just Seventeen* cannot predict who you'll marry or help you fix your nose. You know what else doesn't need fixing? Yup, your hair. Because despite what all those dodgy adverts suggest ... *you're worth it too!*

I know what you're thinking (I'm you, remember!).You're thinking about that morning at the age of nine when mum had finally had enough of you taking forever to do your hair and followed through on her promise to chop it off. You had to sneak into assembly with your hair looking like a lopsided rug. It felt like every eye was following your every move and as your belly filled with shame, you knew you were never going to survive primary school. You realised that day that there was something very wrong with your hair. So wrong that even your own mother didn't want to deal with it anymore. Well, I have something to tell you ...

You are STILL not your hair.

Also, you're going to have to forgive mum 'cause as crazy as it might sound, she's just as clueless as you about how to look after Afro hair. In fact, she's got it worse because she has to pretend like she knows what she's doing. So cut her some slack. You've seen grandma's hair. Mum never stood a chance either. You're still sceptical, I can tell. Now you're thinking about your first school trip in year six. You'd run out of hair moisturiser and had to go away for a week – far from any Afro hair shops. You're remembering the puzzled and horrified stares of your classmates and the itchy feeling of being in your own skin. Like you were defective or something. You couldn't enjoy your first time away from home, all because your hair was dry and sticking up in every direction. The battle that raged inside you that week still makes me sad to this day. So, when I tell you this — please believe that I understand.

You are not your hair.

Not even when your scalp burns from re-touching your roots every six weeks. Or when the braider says your hair is tough or difficult, even as your scalp is stinging beneath her hard hands. It is still true when you're worrying about the weather or dreading your swimming lesson, because you know your hair is going to pouf up. Remember it when you suspect deep down that the reason Luke doesn't like you back is because your hair doesn't swish or swoosh. Or when you have to stand back while your friends try on all those crappy hair accessories that you know will rip through your new growth.

There will always be something or someone trying to make you feel bad about your hair – just as they've been trying to do with every other part of a woman's body since the beginning of time. Whether it's product manufacturers declaring you need to tame your curls, or magazines, movies and TV shows that only seem to value the smooth, straight and silky. It may even be a school's outdated and discriminatory uniform policy or maybe the social media influencer with 'good' hair and a banging braid-out, making you feel less than, because your curls don't look like hers.

So, you need to always know that ...

You
are
not
your
hair.

YYou need to remember those other, happier moments, such as when Folu took pity on you and braided your hair. Those rare flashes of sisterly peace where you sat between her knees, bonded by an act far older than your sibling-esque dislike of each other. Or the nod of understanding, shared across the playground between two black girls who know the joys of getting those baby hairs laid just right. And don't forget the euphoria of using your straighteners without once burning an ear or your forehead.

So, whether you choose to wear your tresses curly in an epic scene-stealing 'fro, Pocahontas bone-straight and swanging, braided to the 'Janet Jackson in *Poetic Justice*' heaven, or covered in a headscarf, silently demanding that the world value your mind before your beauty, just let that choice be yours and not one born out of fear. A fear of not being accepted, a fear of not fitting in or even just fear that you don't have the 'right' texture.

I'll let you in on a little secret. No one has the 'right' texture! You only have *your* texture and it is beautiful. I know you don't believe it right now, but your hair truly is a beautiful thing. It is a unique confection of coils, kinks and curls that echo the intricate dance black women have been doing since the beginning of time.

I wish I didn't need to send you this message – that the negative perceptions that plague Afro hair, just like the tiny 'Fairy Knots' that weave through our strands, didn't exist. I wish I could say things are different now. They're not, but it is getting better.

There's still so much to be done and guess what ... you're going to be a part of that work.

We exist in a moment in time that doesn't understand Black bodies and so denigrates them. But it wasn't always this way. From the length and breadth of pre-colonial Africa, our hair was celebrated, nurtured and beloved and that time will come again soon. You're going to go on a journey of discovery that starts with a simple goal ... to grow long hair. But along the way, you'll begin to ask bigger questions, such as 'How do we break the cycle of hair-hate that follows Black girls and women everywhere they go?'

You'll have to unlearn everything you think you know about yourself and your place in this world. Your hair is just the tip of the iceberg. It isn't going to be easy, but it will be worth it. There will come a time where you will willingly ditch the relaxer and embrace your natural kinks and curls. You will set aside length as a measure of your femininity and sleek smoothness as an indication of your value. You will happily walk into a barber's shop and demand your monthly tapered cut. You will even confidently do the school run with your hair uncombed and zero eyebrows. Sorry, I still haven't managed to grow them back in properly after your little mishap with the tweezers.

You're going to reclaim your **freedom**:

Freedom from the belief that the strands of hair on your head are somehow inferior because they don't conform to the Western standards of beauty.

Freedom from the never-ending cycle of 'miracle' products touted to fix everything from world peace to global warming.

Freedom from feeling you have to prove anything to anyone about the way your hair looks in all its natural glory.

You are going to inspire those closest to you and beyond to embrace their coil-y locks. To move beyond the lies history has fed us and re-discover the beauty of Afro hair. I don't want to give away any spoilers, but it involves books.

Oh, sod it, Girl ... you're going to be an author and your books are going to have an impact. Especially on your own daughters and their sense of self-worth.

Until then, lean into the discomfort of never quite fitting in. You don't need to, And that pain will be what fuels you to make things better. Know that those feelings of frustration and despair with your hair will eventually fade as you learn what it wants and needs. Trust me, it's all going to make sense real soon.

Teenage Tọlá, you are not your hair, but your hair will become a huge part of who you are. I can't wait to meet you there.

Love Tọlá x

WHAT IS CONSENT? SOMA SARA, CONSENT CAMPAIGNER

This may seem like a simple question with an obvious answer. But you'd be surprised by how many people don't actually understand what 'consent' means. Understanding consent is integral to exploring your body space safely and engaging in any kind of healthy relationship. Consent is needed for any intimate activity such as hugging, kissing, holding hands, sharing information, any kind of touching and or even entering someone's physical space. It's important to have a comprehensive understanding of consent; we should know what it is, what it looks like, and how to spot it.

Always remember that consent is yours to give and take away at any time. There's nothing wrong with taking things slowly – find your own pace that's right for you. You are your own person; you don't need to compare yourself or your experiences to others. Trust your gut, and you'll know when you're ready.

And when thinking about consent you might want to ask yourself...

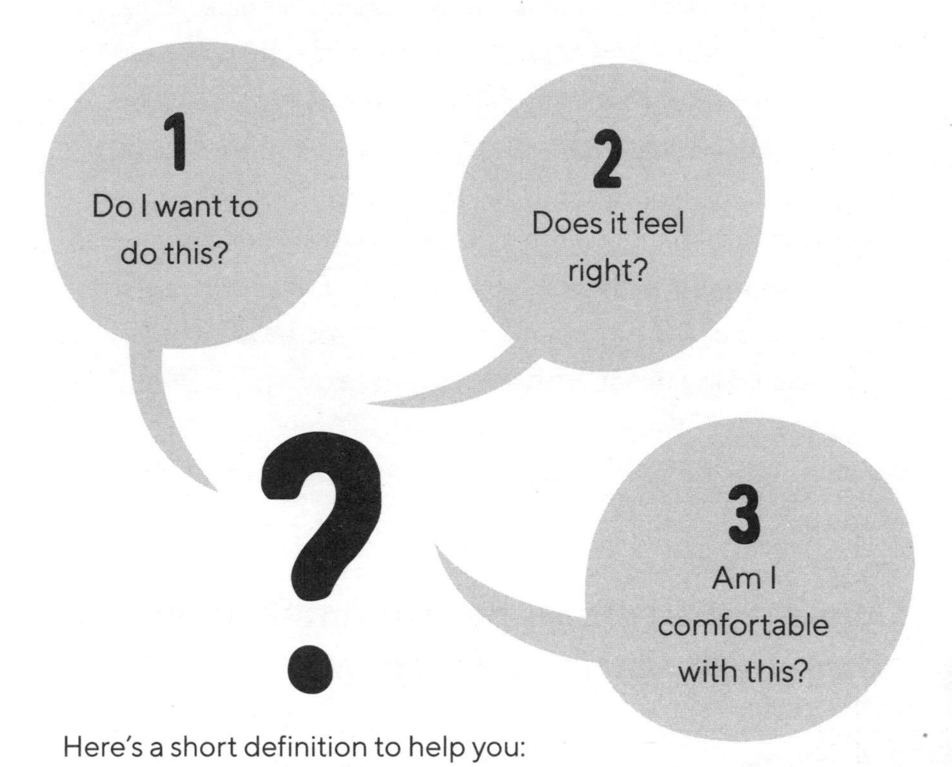

Here's a short definition to help you:

Consent is the **voluntary agreement** to take part in something. This definition applies to hand holding, hugging, massaging someone's shoulders or any kind of touching at all really – and remains the same for consenting to sexual activities.

Someone consents to sexual activity if s/he agrees by choice and has the **freedom** and capacity to make that choice. Note the words 'freedom' and 'capacity' here. If someone is not awake or fully awake, or is under the influence of alcohol or drugs then they're incapable of giving consent.

And remember that consenting to sexual activity may be given to **one sort of sexual activity** but not **another.** For example, giving your consent to kissing does not mean that you have given your consent to taking things further or having sex.

And also remember, you have the right to **withdraw** your consent at any time!

Consent must always be: Informed, freely given, enthusiastic, and ongoing.

It doesn't matter what gender you are, or whether you're straight, gay, or bisexual, if you're planning to engage in any intimate activity then both you and your partner must give consent. In any intimate scenario, it's key that you're attentive and aware of the other person's feelings, desires and well-being. Sometimes you might feel under pressure or even guilty for saying no. If your partner is making you feel this way, know that this is wrong. Sex, when you're ready, and at the legal age, should be about mutual enjoyment, pleasure and consent.

So how does consent work?

There is a misconception that consent can be awkward or could 'ruin the mood'. This is far from the truth because consent allows two people in any kind of relationship to communicate more freely about what they want/don't want and what they like.

Consent can look like...

Communicating freely every step of the way. For example, asking if it's OK to remove an item of clothing or asking if they are ok. Don't make any assumptions, instead check in – ask them how they feel.

Consent is a clear, confident, and enthusiastic 'YES'.

And remember to respect your partner if they say no; they have every right to stop at any moment during any sexual activity. And if you want to stop at any point you can too! Never be afraid to voice how you're feeling in any intimate setting. Don't be afraid to explore what you enjoy because your pleasure matters too! Your sexual agency is important; sex should be about mutual enjoyment; it shouldn't be one sided. Sex should be enjoyable and fun. You are not a passive recipient, you can also initiate relationships, flirting, dating, and sexual interactions too!

Consent can sound like ...

Can I hold your hand?

Can I borrow your phone?

Can I give you a hug?

Do you want to [fill in blank]?

Is this comfortable for you?

Do you like this?

Is this ok?

Would you like me to stop?

That feels amazing!

Do you want to go any further?

I like when [fill in the blank], would you like to do that?

Consent is not ...

The absence of 'no'

Flirting, being nice

Clothing and appearance: what you're wearing is not an indication of whether you want to take anything further than you want to

Feeling so uncomfortable or guilty that you say 'yes'

The fact that you consented before

Being in a relationship: consent is required every time, even in a relationship

Convincing or coercion: 'you'll give me blue balls' 'you're frigid if you don't'

Consenting to one thing does not mean you consent to everything

Unclear or 'ambiguous': if the person is unable to communicate clearly or does not have the capacity to communicate then this is not consent

If it doesn't feel right, it probably isn't. Never forget that your body is yours and no one else's, don't let anyone push you to doing anything that you're not ready for. Never be afraid to say no if you're uncomfortable, or to let your partner know if you're in any pain. Sex should not be painful, don't just 'grin and bear it'.

Always be assertive if you're uncomfortable, speak up, call it out. This might sound like...

If you have an experience of harassment, abuse, coercion, assault, or rape, know that there is always someone to talk to. Whether it is a close friend, someone in your family, or someone on a support line, please know that the act of sharing your experience has helped many. There are many ways to find support if you are struggling with an experience, please visit the Everyone's Invited website to find a list of charities, helplines and resources. You should never be ashamed or feel guilty for what you've been through. If anything's ever happened to you, please know that you are not alone in your experience.

Despite what many might think, consent isn't hard to get your head around. Consent is about establishing and maintaining your own boundaries as well as respecting the boundaries of others. Practicing empathy is key, always be conscious of others and how they might be feeling. Always be kind to others but most importantly be kind to yourself!

SAVING OUR PLANET TOGETHER, DAISY JEFFREY, CLIMATE CHANGE ACTIVIST

Hiya, my name is Daisy and I'm an 18 year old Australian activist fighting for climate justice, amongst other things. I used to feel like my voice didn't matter, like I couldn't make a difference to causes that I cared about, but now having spent three years working as a youth activist, I'm here to tell you about the climate crisis and how

you're never too small to make an impact.

I first became aware of the concept of global warming when I was ten, but only really started being aware of climate change in 2016 when I was 14. We all want to make a difference, but as individuals often feel powerless to effect change. As a school student, I felt there was no way I could

even make the tiniest difference, but when I heard about Greta Thunberg and the school strikes in 2018, I knew I had to get involved. Since then, I've been part of a team that, in 2019, drew crowds of 300,000 to the streets all over Australia to demand climate justice; I've written a book – oh, and I've experienced massive burnout..

So, what is the climate crisis?

Who does it affect?

And how did young people end up being stuck with the job of advocating for science?

First off the bat, the climate crisis is an existential threat to all living things. Simply put, the Earth is heating up very quickly and this warming has been driven largely by the ongoing repercussions of the Industrial Revolution in the 18th cen but that the rate of change we are experiencing is abnormally quick when compared with the average rate of change over millions of years. How did this change happen? The quick answer is that the excessive amount of greenhouse gases we're contributing to the atmosphere over time is causing the planet to heat dramatically.

Do we have solutions to this crisis?

Yes!!! The problem is the lack of political will to take the drastic action now required. Young people did not cause the climate crisis and it certainly should not fall upon us to solve it. In fact, the world's political leaders and corporations have known about the threat of global warming for over three decades, but deliberate political division perpetuated by those with vested interests has resulted in this generation bearing the burden of fighting for their own future.

We are facing a climate crisis, the ramifications of which current generations across the globe are already struggling to overcome. We now have *less than a decade* to drastically take action to mitigate this problem before it's too late. This crisis affects everyone, but it does not affect everybody equally. We know that it will first and foremost hurt women, especially women of colour and indigenous women. I live in Sydney, Australia, and in the summer of 2019–20, I would wake up and walk outside to orange skies and falling ash from the ferocious fires just outside the city. Nearly 500 people and over a billion species of wildlife died either as a direct result of those fires or bushfire smoke inhalation.

It was during those few months that I myself experienced massive burnout. I'd just come back from the 25th Conference of the Parties – the annual conference where political leaders draw up agreements such as the Paris Climate Agreement – and I'd seen diplomats try and fail to take any meaningful steps in the right direction. I'd also witnessed my own government deny that it needed to do any more to address the climate crisis, while our country burned.

I was supposed to be finishing the manuscript for a book called On Hope, but how could I write a book about hope when I didn't have any? Well, in those few months we started to see tens of thousands of people take to the streets at incredibly short notice to demand drastic action be taken to address the crisis. Australians, as a broad generalisation, take pride in not being political, so these protests were a huge demonstration of public opinion in favour of climate justice.

But then the pandemic ...

People worry about what directly impacts their lives and the Covid-19 pandemic has understandably been most people's primary concern. To keep everyone as safe as possible from the virus, we haven't been able to hold huge in-person protests, so the movement has largely moved online which, as much as we'd like it to, does not have the same visual impact as thousands of people taking to the streets.

So, what can we all do to make an impact?

There are multiple things that we, as individuals, can do to make a difference. We can commit to having a smaller carbon footprint. Ways in which we can achieve this are by dietary changes such as going vegan or vegetarian, looking at the companies we source goods from and choosing ethical options instead, that minimise waste etc. But it's crucial to remember that these actions are not accessible to everyone. The most effective answer is to join the climate movement and if you're of voting age, vote for a political candidate who supports ambitious climate action. This is not to say that individual lifestyle changes aren't incredibly important, but the narrative that each individual needs to change their lifestyle, rather than the 100 corporations that contribute to 70% of emissions worldwide, is a bit nuts.

Young women are leading the youth climate movement across the globe. You don't need to be a confident public speaker or have all the time in the world to devote to the cause to make a difference. The first step to joining the climate movement is to find your local chapter of the youth climate movement and send them a message. If there's no local group in your area, you can be the one to start it! It's daunting, but I promise it's worth it!

It's important to remember that no one is perfect .We're all trying our best to create meaningful change and

This year is the 26th Conference of the Parties. The next big agreement since the Paris Climate Agreement will hopefully be reached and to succeed, we all need to come together to fight for a safer future.

Hope requires taking action and, you never know, your voice could be the one that makes all the difference in the world.

EMMA GONZALEZ
GUN CONTROL ACTIVIST

LOVE
TRANS RIGHTS
HOPE
BLACK
LIVE
'Adults like us when we have strong test scores, but they hate us when we have strong opinions'

Teenage girls have the power to change the world, and you, yes YOU, reading this sentence right now, have the power to make a difference on this floating rock we call home. And we need no more proof of the explosive potential of young women, than the dynamite activist Emma Gonzalez.

Emma was just a regular high school student who headed up her school's GSA (gay straight alliance) and was enjoying her teenage years when on Valentine's Day 2018, a mass shooter killed 17 people at her school in Parkland, Florida, sadly becoming the worst school shooting in the history of America.

When met with grief, we all react differently and today when something horrific and desperately wrong occurs we are seeing more and more young women vow to make change and stand up for causes around the world. Emma Gonzalez was no different.

Emma channelled her grief into activism and, along with her friends, she co-founded the gun control advocacy group Never Again MSD who organised the March for Our Lives protest in Washington DC. The biggest youth-led protest since the Vietnam War era, an estimated 200,000 people turned out to march in support of gun control. At the age of 18, Emma Gonzalez gave an emotional but eloquent speech that went viral around the world, protesting about the inaction of politicians who are funded by the NRA (National Rifle Association).

The March for Our Lives protest marked a turning point in America's dialogue around firearms, and because of it, safer gun laws were passed in states across the whole of the US. These included establishing a higher minimum age for buying firearms, and extending the time it takes to acquire them. Not only that, it cemented student activists as leaders in the gun safety movement.

Emma continues to be an activist today. She has launched a March for Our Lives zine, *Unquiet* which is focused on using your voice for the greater good and continues to act in the interest of her local community by helping to instigate real change.

So, who says you can't change the world? If there's something you believe in, your voice is the most powerful tool you have and, as Emma proves,

you are never

too young

to make a difference.

DEAR YOUNGER SELF, YOU ARE STRONG, POWERFUL & INDEPENDENT & I LOVE YOU: A LETTER TO THE YOUNG ACTIVISTS IN ALL OF US, **EVERYDAY RACISM**

NATALIE & NAOMI EVANS

You won't know it yet, but the feeling burning in your chest you had when that person in the school playground said they didn't want to play with you because you looked dirty, will fade.

That they said *that* to you says far more about *them* than it does about you.

One day you will learn to love the colour of your skin. You are 12. You are proud of being you. You are proud of being mixed race; love telling people that your Dad was from Jamaica, and love your Jamaican culture. You love the music, and especially the food, though you'll be a vegetarian in the very near future and will have to learn a whole new way to enjoy it.

And while you wait for the burning in your chest to fade, this comment has you striving to look like the other girls in your year. Wanting to change your hair and eye colour because you don't want to stand out. You won't have the words for it, and so I have written this to tell you... That feeling burning in your chest that the comment caused; that desire to blend in due to the belief that you are too different and somehow lesser – is the feeling of being *othered*.

You will feel better, but it's a journey. This journey is going to be really hard for you, because there will be times when you are going to hate yourself deeply and compare yourself to everyone else. It will get to the point that you will forget to notice how amazing you already are. But guess what? So many wonderful things are going to happen to you! You're going to find strength and beauty in yourself, and you will go on to do the most brave and incredible things. You're going to go on a year-long journey and travel the world all by yourself. You're going to meet people who challenge you as well as some of the most inspiring and kindest people along the way. You're going to get a great job and go on tours across the country, you're going to make such loyal friends, ones who will help you on your own journey of self-acceptance. You're going to write. Failure will become your best friend but trust me when I say there is nothing you won't be able to do.

You are strong, powerful, and independent and I love you.

Now, you are 16 and just about to take your GCSEs. You haven't revised or studied for these exams because you didn't think you were smart enough and you were embarrassed. To your mind, failing them on purpose meant that you had control over the results. You are very smart. You are very perceptive. You are also dyslexic, you'll find this out years later and everything will suddenly have a whole new meaning. You have had a really hard time at school. Making it into the 'popular group' was to your detriment, and you compromised on who you are just trying to fit in.

If I remember correctly, you are already on your third diet, still hating your hips and bum and the fact that you are a bigger size than the other girls in your class. Straightening your hair and wearing so much make-up is helping you get through, but it won't change anything until you learn to love yourself without it too. I am so sorry you couldn't be yourself at school, for the harm you caused yourself and others in the process. It will haunt you forever that you didn't stick up for the girl who wasn't wearing designer shoes when everyone laughed, but once you start loving your differences, you'll want to make sure the world is a fairer place for everyone. Finding your voice was hard, but you'll have a moment as an adult where you realise that defending someone else's right to be safe may mean being visible – and you'll never look back.

You won't always crave attention, you won't strive for people to like you forever, and after many, many diets and toxic relationships with food you will learn to enjoy food and not worry about what others think of you. You will be FREE. You didn't get the grades you wanted at school, but you continued to work hard, went back later (I know, but you will want to I promise!) and got the qualifications you needed to apply for university. You are now fighting injustice, and you run a huge social media platform that fights for equality for all and you're writing a book with your sister.

Through all your faults and regrets you become strong, powerful, and independent and I love you.

I have some news for you. You've just turned 28. Next year will be life-changing even though you are completely unaware of it. You're going to go to work, and on this day, you'll decide to get the train instead of driving, and this little decision will change the trajectory of your life forever – as the little ones often do. You'll witness a racist incident on this train, but instead of just watching, something in you will snap. The train will be absolutely packed but not one person will say a word to defend the ticket conductor as he is racially abused by two men without a ticket. That burning in your chest will come back and you are going to use it to be an active bystander. The words will come, loud but calm and completely unrehearsed. You will say everything you need to say so clearly that the men who were racist apologise for what they had said – and you will remember to record it on your mobile phone (yes we can do that now, it's brilliant). Once you're off the train, you speak with your sister and together you decide that something must be done to stop incidents like that from happening. That one small piece of activism – speaking up for someone else – can make a huge difference.

A few months later you decide to upload this video on social media, to help educate your friends and family that racism does happen in the UK and it's not just an American issue. The video will go viral with over a million people watching it. That is when you realise it is time to make a far bigger statement. That is when you decide to create that safe space for black and brown people, somewhere to share stories of racist incidents that happen in the UK. It won't be long before an awful, awful murder happens in America that sparks the biggest civil rights movement of our lifetime. This is the murder of George Floyd, a black American man who was killed by the police. The world suddenly seems to recognise that racism is more than just calling someone a bad name – that it's systemic and we must become anti-racist in order to dismantle it. As people look for more ways to be an activist in their own everyday lives, the social media platform you created will grow dramatically, and you will have 150,000 people following you. This platform will help people's journey in anti-racism work, they will learn so much from you and your sister, as you both create resources on how to talk about race, how to respond to race comments and how to be an active bystander.

Remember to pace yourself. Even though this all sounds incredible, activism can also be very overwhelming and triggering, and you are going to have some really difficult conversations with your friends, family and strangers about racism. You are going to explore more about your own identity, learning the privilege that you hold and learning to use your privilege to make change. You will struggle with imposter syndrome but you will challenge yourself every day in spite of it.

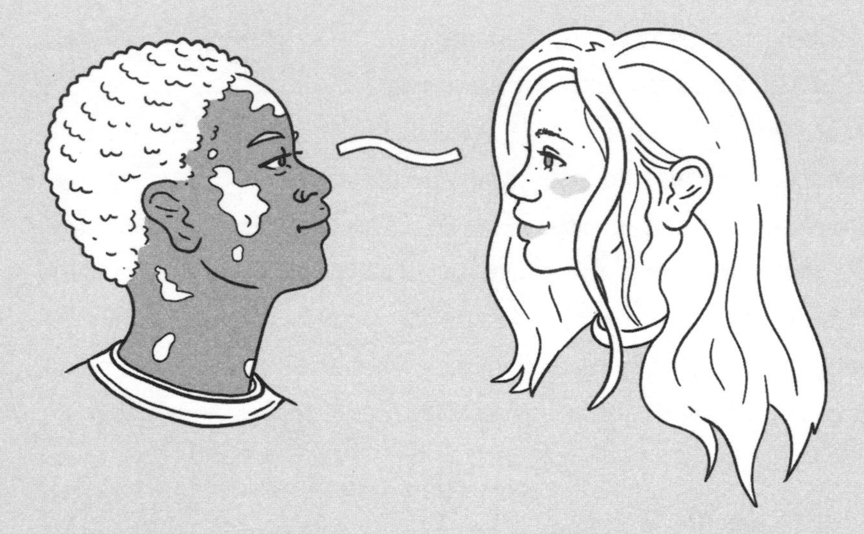

On top of all of this, there is going to be a global pandemic, where we will be in lockdown. You are going to lose your job of five years, but you will find a new job where they value you as an individual and respect your voice. You will buy your first home. Your platform will open up opportunities for you. You are going to write articles for national magazines, even though you hated writing at school, and you are going to be asked to speak in public about your activism. You are going to deliver anti-racism talks for different organisations and companies. You will feel a sense of purpose in a way you never have before and you are going to feel unstoppable.

You are strong, powerful and independent and I love you

10 RULES FOR FINDING YOUR STYLE, HARRIET BYCZOK, STYLIST

RULE 1: MAKE FASHION FUN

Your teenage years are for experimentation, so go a bit wild, and play around with colourful and exciting trends. Have fun finding out what feels most YOU and take some time to try on everything – even pieces that may usually be outside of your comfort zone?

RULE 2: CULTIVATE YOUR INDIVIDUALITY

By all means, borrow ideas from other people's looks but try to find your own truly personal style. How, I hear you ask? My advice is to start by only wearing clothes that you adore – and that you feel truly confident in. This will help you on the road to developing your own personal style. Don't feel you need to follow trends slavishly. Your wardrobe doesn't need to be 'trendy'. Trends can be fleeting, and can come and go so quickly – and can also be expensive (see Rule 8!) so find the trends that work for you and invest in key pieces that last.

RULE 3: BUILD A MOODBOARD

One of the first things I do when working with a new client is I ask them to send me pictures of clothes that inspire them from films, magazines, catwalks – even shop windows – which allows me to see common themes in their favourite pieces. I also ask them to consider style icons from the past and present. For me, some of the most classic looks around were inspired by film and if you're looking for longevity in your wardrobe, look at the classic style icons, such as Bridget Bardot or Audrey Hepburn. Once I have gathered all this style 'evidence' I make an inspiration folder online so that my client and I can reference those looks when pulling pieces from designers. Why don't you try putting together a mood board for yourself?

RULE 4: WEAR STUFF THAT MAKES YOU FEEL BADASS

Fashion is an expression of your personality, so take time to reflect on what your clothes say about you. Trust your taste. If you wear an outfit that makes you feel confident and badass, break down what it is that makes you feel this way and incorporate more of these looks into your wardrobe. For example, if wearing a floaty, floral dress with a pair of Dr Martens makes you feel on top of the world, try to bring that aesthetic into the rest of your wardrobe.

RULE 5: IT DOESN'T HAVE TO BE EXPENSIVE

Looking good doesn't have to be expensive, especially when experimenting and finding your style. Quality over quantity is my mantra! Having a few key pieces you can mix and match makes putting outfits together a lot easier than buying things on a whim that will end up languishing in your wardrobe (and cluttering it up – see Rule 6). Don't rule out a classic look if it works for you. So, if jeans, a T-shirt and a pair of loafers are your thing, and makes you feel badass (see Rule 4) then work with variations of that and make it your 'look'.

RULE 6: DECLUTTER YOUR WARDROBE

Keeping a minimal, decluttered and organised wardrobe saves you time and money. Once the weather starts to change I store away clothes that are off-season, this way I have no distractions and can easily navigate through my closet. Another great tip is grouping pieces together by type (bottoms, tops, dresses etc) so styling a look is made easier, then at the start of the week, I look at the weather and what I have planned for the week and put together outfits, this way when I am in a hurry I am not grabbing the same thing and forgetting about all the other gems I have hidden.

RULE 7: DRESS FOR YOUR LIFESTYLE

Comfort is everything. Let's face it, there's nothing worse than not being able to walk properly because your shoes hurt or move freely because your trousers are too tight. I love dressing up and wearing heels and a fitted dress but sometimes it's nice to have the comfort and freedom of wearing leggings and trainers so I can run for the bus. Casual clothes have come a long way so you can still look great and feel comfortable. Think about what you do on a day-to-day basis and build your wardrobe to work best with your routine and your lifestyle. Comfort breeds confidence in my book!

RULE 8: ACCESSORISE, ACCESSORISE, ACCESSORISE!

To my mind belts, shoes, bags, scarves and jewellery are what make clothes an outfit, and can really make your look personal to you. So invest in some accessories. A great belt or neck scarf can transform a plain dress or a pair of jeans. And accessories don't have to be expensive (see Rule 5). Trawl charity shops, vintage shops and jumble sales for great belts, scarves and evening bags – or even raid your mum's/gran's wardrobe (ask them first, of course!).

RULE 9: BE AN ECO FASHIONISTA

Whenever possible I try to shop vintage or second-hand. Charity shops are great for a bargain (visit them regularly to swoop the best pieces) or swap/share clothes with your friends. You may need to alter clothes that you buy second-hand, but if you love a piece, and the material and the cut are amazing, it is always worth getting it professionally altered to fit your shape and size. If you are handy with a needle or sewing machine (a great skill to have as a fashion lover!) make it your own and alter it yourself. Of course, you're going to outgrow some of your pieces but don't throw them away; donate them, recycle them or wash, repair and sell them. One woman's trash is another woman's treasure, as the saying goes!

RULE 10: STOCK UP ON BASICS

This is a much-overlooked rule of fashion, but one of my favourite bits of advice. Have a good stash of basic, but decent quality, T-shirts and shoes that go with everything. Trust me, it will work wonders for your stress levels! A handful of good white and black T-shirts will go with pretty much everything and can balance out prints, meaning you can put together outfits more quickly and easily! Win-win.

Fashion icons are icons because they break rules so express yourself, be unapologetic and laugh at your mistakes. Enjoy the art of fashion and the process, and most importantly, always remember to stay true to yourself.

STEPPING INTO MY POWER, ELLEN JONES, LGBTQ+ RIGHTS CAMPAIGNER

If you skip this bit entirely, know this: I was the weird, nerdy gay kid with severe depression and few friends, and yet, my life has become something beyond my wildest imagination ...

Growing up, my existence always felt at odds with the universe. With every year that passed, I would feel more at odds with the world. This probably came across, at the time, that I thought I was 'not like other girls,' a sentiment I loathed then and still do now. In reality, I was queer and autistic – and both of those things did, in fact, make me different to most of the girls around me. I just didn't know it at the time.

I came out when I was 14 years old, which surprises many people because it seems young. Granted, they are not as surprised as I was, given that I learned that lesbians existed not through any comprehensive PSHE curriculum, or from role models in the media, but from the beloved comedy classic *The Vicar of Dibley*.

Since then I've noticed that, as a rule, people tend to normalise 'progress' fairly quickly. Take the surge of queer and trans representation in recent years – it's easy to forget that as a person born in 1998, I did not grow up with gay role models. Incidentally, growing up, there were also very few 'Ellens' my age. It was only as an adult I found out that when Ellen Degeneres came out the name soared in popularity.

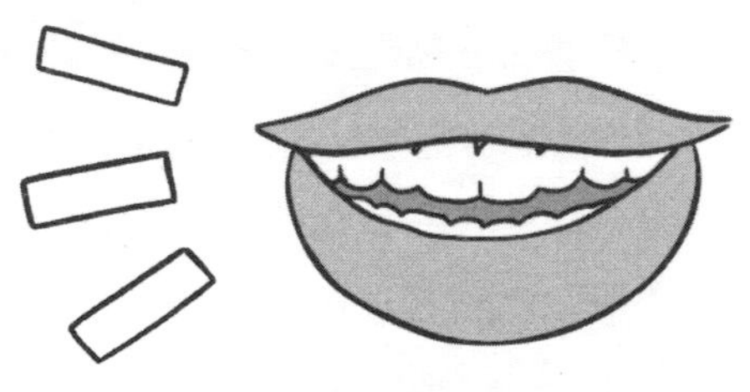

Put simply, when I was born, being gay was not a good thing to be. Growing up, I didn't have an opinion on gay people because I simply did not know they existed. When I realised I was gay, I had no real feelings about it, other than intense uneasiness and fear about the uncertainty of what would happen next. I had also absorbed – through what little info I could find – that queer people often had sad, lonely, hard lives.

With the benefit of hindsight, I can see that this is not about being queer, but because queer people experience horrific oppression and prejudice. But at the time I felt like I was the problem. I would fall asleep sobbing wishing someone could make me straight; make me 'normal'.

And that was before the online death threats started.

In all, I endured about 18 months of messages telling me to do all manner of self-destructive things for being gay. Sometimes, six or seven times a day. The messages always had identifying features that meant they could only have come from one of my schoolmates and so, naturally, I confided in a trusted teacher who was responsible for pastoral care at my school.

At the time the best advice they could give me was to come offline. I felt like the message was that this was something I should just get used to.

But let me be perfectly clear. You never have to *get used* to abuse.

Sugar-coating this period in my life would be pointless. It was bleak. I was depressed, self-harming, engaging in disordered eating behaviours and no one knew because I had stopped talking about it. How could I talk about something I thought I deserved – for being gay – and that I'd been told to expect?

Being able to heal from all this meant first getting extraordinarily angry. Was that anger always healthy? Not necessarily. But it did help me feel like I was doing something to take control of the situation. I started using my newfound anger and subsequent drive to make connections and work out what should have been done differently – and why that didn't happen.

This was the start of my work building a better world for the LGBTQ+ community.

My aim was to build the community I did not have, and a support infrastructure that could provide safety and stability. It started at school by just creating a group which met once a week. At the first meeting there was a grand total of three of us. By the time I left Sixth Form two years later, we had 40 regular members and all sorts of people popping in and out as they needed.

I am a firm believer that tea and biscuits will not save the world on their own, but it's a very good start.

What I was doing wasn't rocket science, but it was making people feel safe. If you can make people feel supported, you can help them to thrive. It meant treating people with compassion, helping them work out what they needed and how that could be implemented. There shouldn't be anything extraordinary about that, but sadly there is.

There is a curveball in the narrative here. If my life were a work of fiction, I would probably be accused of using an unrealistic plot device. Getting diagnosed as autistic at 19 changed my life in every conceivable way because it not only explained what others had termed my 'weirdness', but it enabled me to find a community of people who had the same experiences.

Lots of people, but girls especially, are autistic but do not get diagnosed. As a result, they go their whole lives not knowing that the way they experience and interact with the world is fundamentally different to those around them, and often at opposition with it.

I learned at a very early age that girls were supposed to be good at socialising and people-pleasing, and that being outspoken or having meltdowns would not be tolerated. My parents raised me in a very gender-neutral way and I suspect this is why, growing up, I was almost two different people: At Home Ellen and At School Ellen.

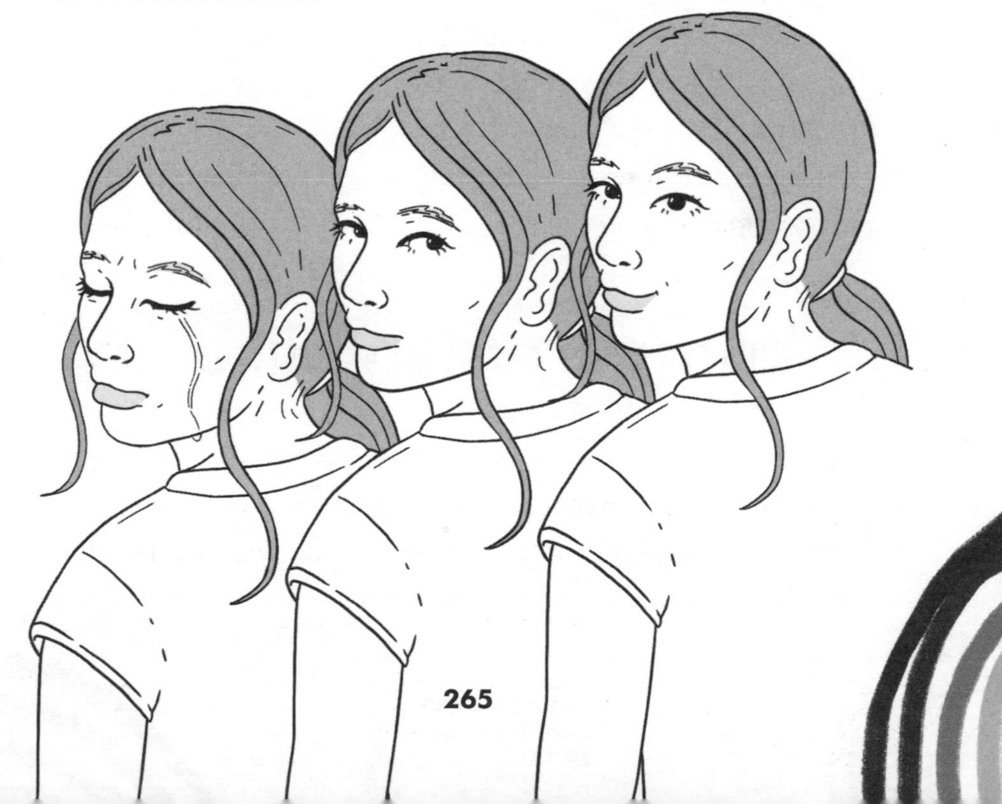

We talk in the autistic community of 'masking', which is just what it sounds like. We put on a mask to help deal with the world. Or rather, the world doesn't accept us and so we are forced to pretend to be something we are not. It's less fun when you phrase it like that. The older I got, the harder masking my autism became. All the world may be a stage, but I am no actress and the constant performance was doing me in. In the same way that pretending to be straight for the sake of society almost destroyed me, masking my autism the whole time was exhausting.

What I found even more excruciating, though, was how often I was expected to

'compart mentalise'

bits of myself to placate others. I have lost opportunities to have my voice heard because I refused to be one thing – either queer or disabled. If people can understand and enjoy the plot of *The Matrix*, surely they can embrace my two separate identities?

Being

'boundaried'

– not only in my work but in my personal life – has been revelatory. It is apparent to me now that my success has been in part because I was used as 'trauma porn'.

I don't regret the work I did, but I do understand now that reliving traumatic experiences to prove the need for inclusion, was not good for my wellbeing. But without it my efforts were going to be fruitless.

Aside from the homophobic and ableist pushback I receive when advocating for my community, the next most frequent criticism was just outright dismissal.

'You can't do that'

or

'Brave of you to think **a girl like you** could change things'.

Often I would be told that we had equality already because gay people could get married. I would find myself responding with the immortal words of my hero Dana Scully, 'I don't have time for your convenient ignorance'. Like my *X-Files* crush, being an outspoken young woman who rocks a suit has often been presented to me – often by men in positions of power – as something 'unladylike' or somehow out of turn.

Although this made situation made me livid, my actual response was curiosity.

Why would you tell a young woman that they were small or weak?

Why would you tell a young woman that they should be quiet and reserved?

You do that out of fear, and to reinforce the status quo.

And as we know from history, women do not have power when the patriarchy is operating as it should. In the past, this was done by confining women to very specific roles both at home and at work. Now, women are told that they cannot possibly create change, that their efforts will be fruitless and so they daren't even try to alter things.

It's a control enacted both through demeaning women and by enforcing gendered ideas about what being a 'good girl'.

As a society, we are still teaching young girls that they should stay in their place. It does not shock me at all that those who most vociferously oppose my work are the ones who have the most to lose. To them, advocating & striving for equity means they will lose the privilege they have become accustomed to. I am a threat to that.

I am still the weird, nerdy gay kid with depression. I am also an autistic lesbian who can't think straight in any capacity. I like terrible puns and British comedy. I can recite to you most episodes of *Doctor Who*, love Radio 4 and recite plays to myself around the house. I'm too scared to ask for things in shops and yet can command a stage in front of thousands of audience members.

I'm the mum-friend, drink an absurd amount of Diet Coke and value the friends who have stuck around like they are family. I'm

loud and **quiet,**

feminine and **masculine,**

bold and **subtle,**

queer and **disabled.**

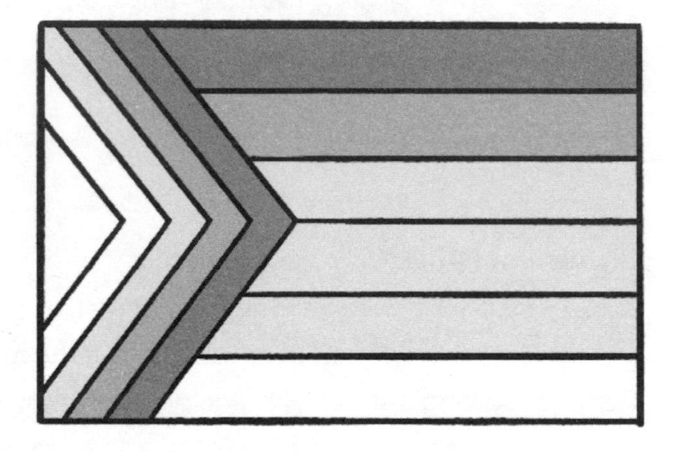

Once upon a time I would have hated myself for being 'too much' for other people.

Now, I refuse to compartmentalise myself, to make myself smaller for others because I do not exist for the consumption of others.

I think they call this character progression.

10 THINGS TO MAKE YOU FEEL GOOD (& DOESN'T INCLUDE BINGEING NETFLIX!)

1 ESCAPE INTO A BOOK

I mean, you're doing it now, so congratulations to you and 10 points to Gryffindor, but below is my list of important books that helped me become who I am today, and, in my opinion, every young woman should read: *The Bell Jar* by Sylvia Plath, *How To Be a Woman* by Caitlin Moran, *The Power* by Naomi Alderman, *Are You There God? It's Me Margaret* by Judy Bloom, *The Hunger Games* by Suzanne Collins, *The Perks of Being a Wallflower* by Stephen Chbosky, *I Know Why the Caged Bird Sings* by Maya Angelou, *To Kill A Mockingbird* by Harper Lee.

2 LIVE YOUR BEST LIFE WITH ... A VISION BOARD!

A vision board is great if it's online, but even better if it's in real life. Flick through old magazines and clip out pictures and print photos off the internet to build a vision board full of things you want to do, see and achieve in the future. It could be what your dream apartment might look like, your goals for the next year, the job you want to have one day. With a vision board you can, quite literally, create the life you want with a collage. And vision boards can really help you to focus on your goals, too, so get clipping!

3 BONJOUR, HOLA, CIAO!

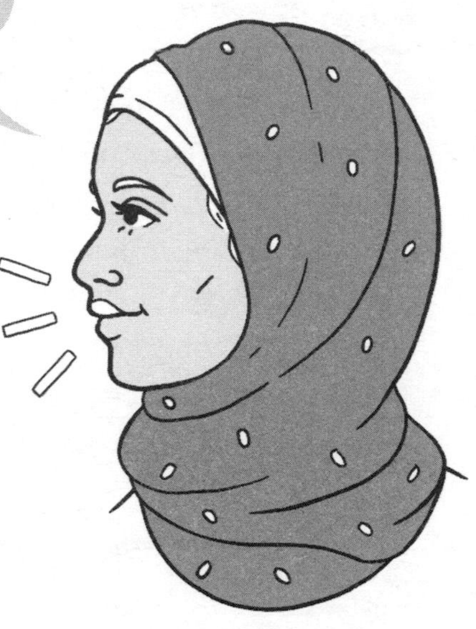

Learning a new language is brilliant for developing your multi-tasking and listening skills and your mental flexibility. And it's so easy now with the help of apps on your phone or online courses. Before long you can be speaking confidently in another language – how great is that? And of course, when you finally make it on an exciting adventure to Paris or Hong Kong or Mexico, you can communicate in the native tongue.

4 COMPLIMENTS TO THE CHEF

Why not give your personal chef a night off, find a recipe for a type of food you've never tried before and get cooking? Maybe try a new style, like vegan or try rolling your own sushi? A skill that will always be useful is learning how to bake a show-stopping birthday cake. That way you'll never be short of a present to give, and everyone loves the person who brings cake to a party. So roll up your sleeves and get cooking up a storm!

5. GET CRAFTY!

Crafting completely took off during the pandemic lockdowns with young people turning to traditional crafts to while away the hours indoors, keep themselves busy and to achieve a level of peace and mindfulness. Sure not all of us can be the next Grayson Perry, but crafting has been shown to ease stress, whether it's sewing, knitting, cross-stitch, embroidery or pottery. As well as all the other benefits, come Christmas or birthdays, homemade things make lovely gifts, too!

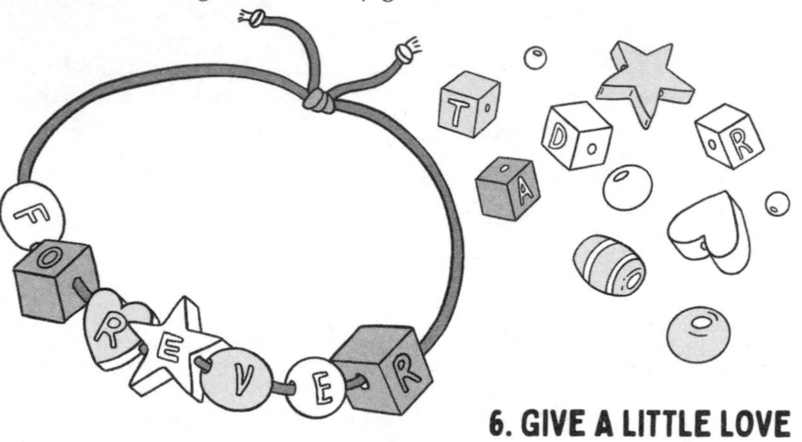

6. GIVE A LITTLE LOVE

Why not try to find a volunteering job locally by approaching a cause that you believe in, or is close to your heart? It could be a kids' activity club, working at a food bank, raising money for charity, offering your time for a few shifts in a charity shop or helping the elderly. Gather up a bunch of your friends and organise bake sales (utilising your new-found cooking skills from number 4 above!), sponsored runs (or silences!) and raise money for a good cause.

7. TIDY ROOM, TIDY MIND?

I don't know if the above saying is true, but I can tell you that tidying up certainly makes me feel A LOT calmer. You don't have to be perfectionist about it, but keeping your space tidy, organised and clean (and, yes, that includes getting stuck annoyingly in your duvet cover when changing your bed!) will help you think more clearly and feel a bit more in control of your life. The life-changing magic of dusting – who knew?

8. EAT THE FROG (OR DO THE HARDEST TASK FIRST!)

Make a list of all the tasks you need to do in a day. It should include the good and the bad, the fun and the boring. Tackle it by doing the toughest stuff first (this is the frog!) Do your work. Do your chores. Do the boring things you hate. I know, I know. I can't believe how dull this sounds either, but get the things you don't want to do out of the way first and that way they don't loom over you. You can spend the rest of your day feeling free as a bird!

9. CLASS ACTION

Hit play and take an online class to learn a new skill. There are thousands of free classes online, from hip-hop to watercolour painting or investing your savings. It's always good, smart and savvy to spend your time learning something new for free!

10. MONEY DOESN'T GROW ON TREES

Earning a bit of extra money is always useful and will make you feel proud of your achievements. Perhaps you could offer your services babysitting to parents/carers in your area? Can you do some extra chores around the house? Washing cars in your neighbourhood can be fun on a sunny day! Can you help tutor younger kids? Or could you build an online shop to sell your craft projects? Start thinking like an entrepreneur and forging good money habits now!

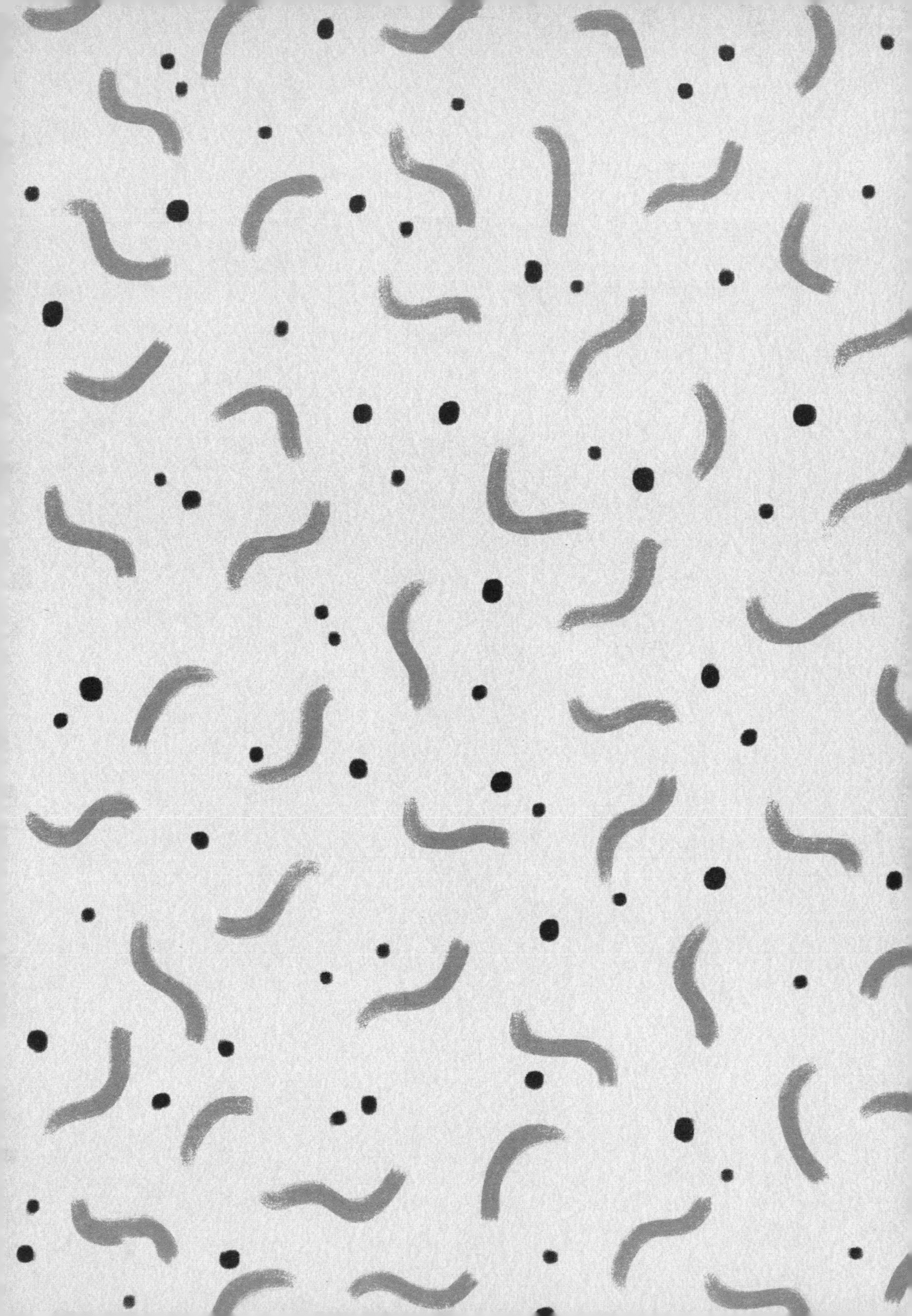

STEP 5

TAKE OVER THE WORLD
TAKING UP SPACE IN THE WORLD AND LOOKING FORWARD TO YOUR FUTURE!

Dear 14-year-old self,

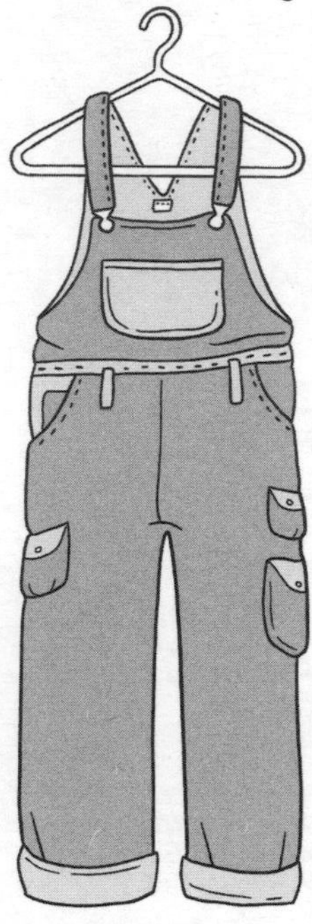

It's me, 25-year-old you! Yes, I know, you thought 25 was horrendously grown-up but it's not, OK? Don't worry, we're still rocking the dungarees and to your utmost joy, you now have red hair, but alas you're not married to Ron Weasley, so your chances of tiny red-haired babies are slim ...

So, what can I tell you? What have I learnt now that I'm SO old and wise? Well, that. It's not wisdom that is bestowed with age, instead it's experiences that usually involve failing in some way.

People still describe us as 'sweet' (which *still* makes us vomit) but let's face it, there are worse things we could be.

So, 14-year-old me, I'm here to remind you to take up space in the world! Why? Because you have as much right as anyone else to be in a room! You don't need permission to exist so stop walking around with your arms crossed; it is not a mode of protection, your body is fine, and you just look permanently cold. And also try not to curl yourself up into a ball. You are not an armadillo.

I know you want to grow up so fast; let face it, 'living in the moment' has never been your strong point, but if you keep waiting for the next exciting thing, you're going to wish your life away. 'Happiness' is not an endpoint, but a feeling that comes and goes, and if you try and chase it, it will elude you! So instead, try and find joy in the little things: the crisp autumn days that you love, the post-ballet class hot chocolates with your best friends, the way your mum always chooses your favourite meals for Saturday night tea.

Try not to idolise people too much. If you put them on too high a pedestal, they will fall off it. No one's perfect; adults don't have it all figured out and may treat you badly sometimes. Be the lead in your own life, not a bit part to someone else's starring role. Have those 'main character moments' and have them often!

Not everyone's going to like you, which is just horrific for a people-pleaser like us, but making a list of people you know for certain don't like you, is not going to help our mental health in any way. Not everyone will share the same moral compass as us, and you can't judge someone for being raised differently. Your heart may get broken, but will be put back together by the people who are always there for you – those you probably overlook sometimes. And that includes your family. Sure, your dad is always on at you to put your clothes away nicely, and your mum has given up trying to tidy your bedroom, it's that bad, but they are your biggest cheerleaders.

Your best friends are there to pick you up off dance studio floors when you're exhausted, and eat Chinese takeaway in bed with – and they always will be.

There will be times, when you're in a big group of people, that you quite literally lose your voice. You will want to join in the conversation but physically no words will come out. Push yourself in there. Yes, you are shy, but you have thoughts that deserve to be listened to.

AND PLEASE STOP SAYING SORRY.

It's been ingrained in women since the dawn of time to apologise for everything, even stuff that isn't our fault! Guilt is an emotion that mucks with your head and you will never do anything bad enough that you should beat yourself up about it for a month. So, stop worrying! I know it's an impossible thing to say, but most of the things you worry about never happen, so you're living through horrid scenarios in your head totally unnecessarily. It's something we need to keep working on even in adulthood, but we'll get there.

You've always known what you've wanted, so keep going, but go easy on yourself, and remember to enjoy it. Look forward to your future, teenage Rosie. But remember, it's not the destination that's important, it's the journey.

Love,

Me xx
P.S You look ACE in those Dr Martens.

> "There's power in allowing yourself to be known and heard, in owning your unique story, in using your authentic voice."
>
> MICHELLE OBAMA

FIND YOUR FUNNY, REBECCA FRONT; ACTOR, WRITER, COMEDIAN

Do me a favour ... Cast your mind back to the last time you laughed. Really laughed, I mean, not some mimsy, polite chuckle, but one of those full-throated, gaspy, weepy, snotty, can't breathe, can't stop, almost painful kind of laughs. Now I want you to recall who it was who made you laugh like that? A friend? A family member? A stranger? And then ask yourself if the instigator of the laugh was male or female?

That might seem like a strange question since any one of any gender can make you laugh. Right?

Well, here's the thing: up until fairly recently, many people would have answered 'no.' For a long, long time there was a belief – seemingly widely held and certainly frequently articulated – that women aren't funny. It feels bizarre seeing it written down like this, but believe it or not, when I first started working in comedy several decades ago, the question I was most often asked in interviews was:

'Are women funny?'

And I would scratch my head and peer into the middle-distance and answer as politely as I could, that yes, women can be funny, as funny as men, and often even funnier. And that speaking as the product of a girls' school and an all-female college, I could vouch for the fact that my education had not been spent in solemn silence, but in an atmosphere of riotous, raucous laughter. And then I'd walk away from the journalist in question and wonder what the hell they'd been doing with their lives that they didn't already *know how funny women are.*

After a while, I noticed that I wasn't being asked that question so often in interviews. I hoped it was because the message had finally got through; that people finally understood that it was idiotic to think that humour was a male preserve. But more likely I wasn't being asked it because I was doing more drama than comedy; and because I was a mother now, and therefore all interviewers were instead obliged to ask 'How do you juggle your career and your family' – another question that's seemingly only ever asked of women.

A couple of years ago, I was invited to address a group of women at my kids' school, and I decided to talk about comedy. By way of research, I messaged a lot of my female friends who work in comedy; really successful women stand-ups, producers, sitcom stars, panellists on primetime shows and writers of hilarious books. I wrote:

You know that question about whether women are funny? That's not a thing any more, right?

Every one of those brilliant, witty women said that not only had they too been asked it repeatedly throughout their careers, but that from time to time they still were.

So where has it come from, this crazy notion? And why is it important that we stamp on it once and for all?

I suspect the root of it lies in ignorance but also in tradition. In previous generations – and to a certain degree today – women and men have lived very different lives. They've been educated separately and expected to follow different paths. Women were often homemakers; men were usually expected to go out to work. Even when women worked too, their jobs were often 'women's' jobs. And after marriage, men and women's social lives were frequently segregated – men went to the pub, women met up in each other's homes, for instance. Think about all those costume dramas, like Downton Abbey, set in grand country houses. What happens as soon as the formal dining finishes? The women leave and the men stay together for coffee and cigars. It's safe to assume that there were as many laughs among the ladies in the drawing room as among the men in the dining room. But the men probably wouldn't have known that. And there are reasons why they might not have wanted to know.

Women have traditionally been prized for their looks, their modesty, their good sense and their compliance. If those are the things that make you an asset, then being funny is going to be considered a disadvantage. It's not 'demure' or 'ladylike'. Being funny might – perish the thought – make you seem 'unattractive'.

So the wit and hilarity that we experience when we are around women must always have been there, but it was at best not noticed and at worst suppressed and discouraged.

In defence of those journalists and their 'Are women funny?' questions, it's easy to see how a male who's grown up around, been educated with, worked predominantly with and socialised only with other males might be surprised to discover that females are every bit as funny as they are!

But why would the myth that women aren't funny *persist*, in a world where we mix so much more freely? Well, I'm afraid I think the answer lies in the P word: Patriarchy. In so many areas of life, this is still predominantly a man's world. Most corporate environments are male dominated; men are still far more widely represented in politics, the media and sport, for example.

Now think about what happens when you make someone laugh – it diffuses tension, it gets you noticed, it highlights the point you are trying to make, it makes you harder to ignore or forget.

Being funny is powerful!

Men have traditionally held the reins of power in our society, but women are already encroaching on that. If men acknowledge we are as funny as they are, they stand to lose even more ground.

So here's my advice to you: whether you are wry, dry, sharp or raucous; or whether you're none of those things but still enjoy laughing and not taking life too seriously. Embrace that. Use it. It is our power every bit as much as it is theirs. Read the mood in the room, of course. No one's suggesting you go into a job interview wearing clown shoes or bust out a 10-minute comedy sketch at a funeral. But never be afraid to make that witty remark, to race towards a punchline, and to be smart, fast, loud and confident when you do.

If you don't say it, one of the guys will and you'll feel like kicking yourself. We've always been hilarious; now's the time to own it.

Find Your Funny, and don't be afraid to use it.

BOUNDLESS BOUNDARIES: HOW TO DRIVE THE COURSE OF LIFE FREELY & SAFELY AS A YOUNG WOMAN,

CIARA CHARTERIS, ACTOR

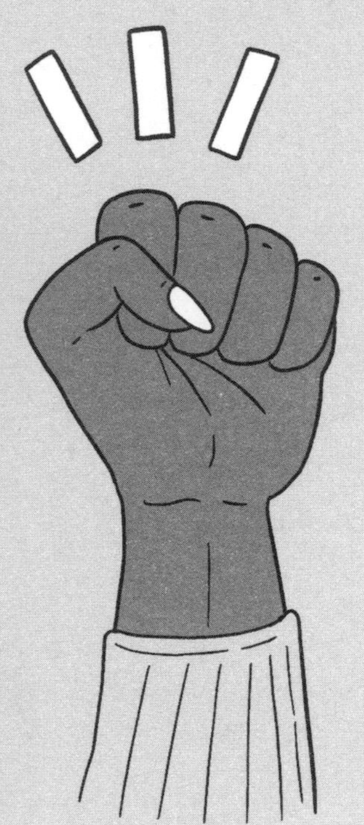

We often think of boundaries as rules; things that hold us back, not move us forward, and rules are made to be broken, right? So why on Earth would we want to live with boundaries? As teenagers this is prime boundary-breaking time, and the overwhelming need to explore your independence, as adulthood becomes tantalisingly close, is exhilarating and important (when not causing stress or fear of course!).

Well actually, I believe that boundaries are your BEST friend in life. Weird right? But go with me!

I have been fascinated by boundaries my whole life, but it has taken me all of 26 years to even begin to understand their power and purpose and feel I have autonomy over them. At school, we are taught that boundaries are restrictions – they reflect the societal standards of life that we are supposed to live by, particularly as girls. From practicalities such as not walking home alone, what we wear, to how we assert ourselves – and if we get these 'wrong' in any way, we should only expect the worse. I used to believe this.

First things first, I want to change the idea of what a boundary is. To do that, we need to understand the difference between a boundary and a restriction. What better way to do this than to use a good old-fashioned dictionary! Below I have put the definitions in for reference. It's so easy to assume that seemingly similar words mean the same thing, but they don't, especially in this case.

Dictionary definition of 'Restriction':

- a limiting condition or measure, especially a legal one.
- the limitation or control of someone or something, or the state of being restricted.

Dictionary definition of 'Boundary':

- a line that marks the limits of an area; a dividing line.
- a limit of something abstract, especially a subject or sphere of activity.

So, for example: one of my personal restrictions is that I am 5ft 2in. This means I can never reach the top shelves without having to do a death-defying counter climb and I always get stuck under someone's armpit on the tube. But *boundaries* – I get to CHOOSE them and implement them for MYSELF. For me, they help to maintain balance, they allow me ultimate freedom with the utmost protection. They are my metaphorical markers, my personal warning bells, they can be private or public, and are unique and fundamental to me. They remind me of my worth and help to demand this from the world around me.

As a woman having boundaries can be exceedingly complicated as they reflect many misconceptions about us, and unfortunately we still don't seem to have the same birthright to freedom and safety that men do. Although this is changing, we have a long way to go before we do. In order to accelerate this change, we must continue to redefine what being a women is by breaking the boundaries previously designed for us by others (men), and get to know ourselves well enough to build new ones that reflect who we truly are and what we want. For as long as we can shape our own boundaries, we too can be free and safe.

I like to think of boundaries like brakes on a car. Your willingness and comfort to use them are your brake lights; they safely alert those around you that right now you're needing to slow down, or stop. To be un-boundaried is to be constantly and consistently speeding. This means we can give too much without realising it and before you know it you've crashed.

Like any new skill,

implementing boundaries takes practice.

The more you practise and explore your boundaries the more capable you are, and the more you get to know your 'vehicle', the more control you ultimately have over it. With boundaries you can still accelerate safely and when necessary (and sometimes it is very necessary!) but it is a choice only you make, and you can safely make it knowing that the brakes are there whenever you need them.

I find my boundaries are usually regulated by my gut. That gut feeling that can happen in an instant, be it discomfort, fear, love, excitement; we all have gut feelings, most of the time without even thinking. These feelings help to signal what boundary may be necessary in any given situation. However, sometimes our gut feeling gets overshadowed by our surroundings, by other people and what they think, what we think, and more often than not, what we *think* we should be thinking.

Before you know it we've talked ourselves right out of that initial gut feeling and our boundaries are lost with it. Now, sometimes this can be a good thing, intellect is important. However, the trick is to try not to allow our brains to talk over our gut, but work with it, both are equally important. Sometimes trusting that gut of yours is even more vital to your safety in the moment. When I trust and listen to my gut, with the help of my boundaries, navigating situations like whether or not I go to a party, or feel uncomfortable sitting on the bus, become infinitely easier.

Many scientists believe our guts are our 'second brain', many of the same neurons and neurotransmitters that are found in our central nervous system are also found there. Therefore, 'gut feelings' play a key part in our communication with ourselves and others. Our gut can help us to react and recognise things that the brain may be too over stimulated to pick up on. To follow our vehicle analogy, the gut would be like your eyes, alerting you to your surroundings, while your boundaries, your brakes, manage just how quickly or slowly you get there. You wouldn't get into a car blindfolded with no brakes, now would you?

It is important to remember that everyone's boundaries are different and some work better for others then they will for you. Life's unfair like that. Your boundaries can look and feel completely different to those of your friends, and that is ok! Don't judge others for theirs, and don't feel judged for yours. You do not have to bend or break your boundaries to be seen, to adjust a boundary is a choice that is only yours to make, and you are free to make them as and when you please. Another bonus, unlike my height, is that

boundaries are not set in stone,

and as you grow and learn so will your boundaries.

As a teenager my boundaries often left me on the outside looking in; to my friends my boundary choices felt like judgements which made them uncomfortable and me lonely. I was the friend everyone wanted in a crisis, but not the one they wanted at their parties. For a while I let this define me, but what I have finally come to realise is that I can have my boundaries AND be the life and soul of a party – but only when I am surrounded by those who respect them, not by those who ask me to break them. I was never the odd one out, I was just always in the wrong environment and I didn't always trust myself enough to leave it. In a comfortable and safe environment, with the right people, your boundaries will never feel like restrictions, in fact you will barely notice they're there. They are just pure, safe, freedom.

Having boundaries should warrant nothing in return but respect and honour from those who truly care for you. This makes them a great tool for calling out those who do not respect you or who may be trying to take advantage of you. Be aware of those who speed through life, un-boundaried, looking as if they are capable of everything but accountable for nothing. They will crash and you do not want to be a part of the collision, no journey is worth it, trust me. It is also not your job to uphold other people's boundaries for them, be that out of fear, or even in protection of them. Your only job is to watch after your own.

I know as teenagers you are all very busy, and there are a lot of voices talking at you, telling you who you are and what you should or shouldn't be doing – friends, family, teachers, the list goes on! So in the moments where the voices, or the setting is too loud to recognise what it is you want, I like to use this 3-point ACT checklist for your very own 'vehicle' and boundary management. A quick-fire way to get your gut and brain talking and kick your boundaries into action.

ACT CHECKLIST:

Assess
Concern?
Turn or Trust

ASSESS

Quickly evaluate the situation by listening to your gut.

CONCERN

Question, is there anything about this that is making you (your gut) uncomfortable, confused? Is there any kind of cause for concern?

TURN

If the answer is YES to the above, turn, walk away, mentally or physically. Most of the time that choice is yours and you can ALWAYS make it.

TRUST

If you feel comfortable or you see no reason to be concerned, then you can BEGIN to trust.

Just know that at any point, with anyone, you can always re-**ACT**.

Now, having said all of that, I must make it clear, that you can't prevent what you can't predict, and you can't predict everything, so know now that you will inevitably trust people you should have turned from, and turn from people you should have trusted. It's the complex and often dark side of being human. Even with all the knowledge and brilliant boundaries, your 'vehicle' is still going to be tested. However, you are the driver of your own life, you choose which roads to take and how you get there. Yes, there will be restrictions along the way and not all those choices will be right at first, but most of them will have a view that offers something beautiful, even when you can't see it.

So build yourself the perfect vehicle for the journey, one with impeccable engineering that can get you to where you want to be.

Be balanced and infinitely boundless, even with boundaries.

BOUNDLESS BOUNDARIES: The perfect juxtaposition to live by.

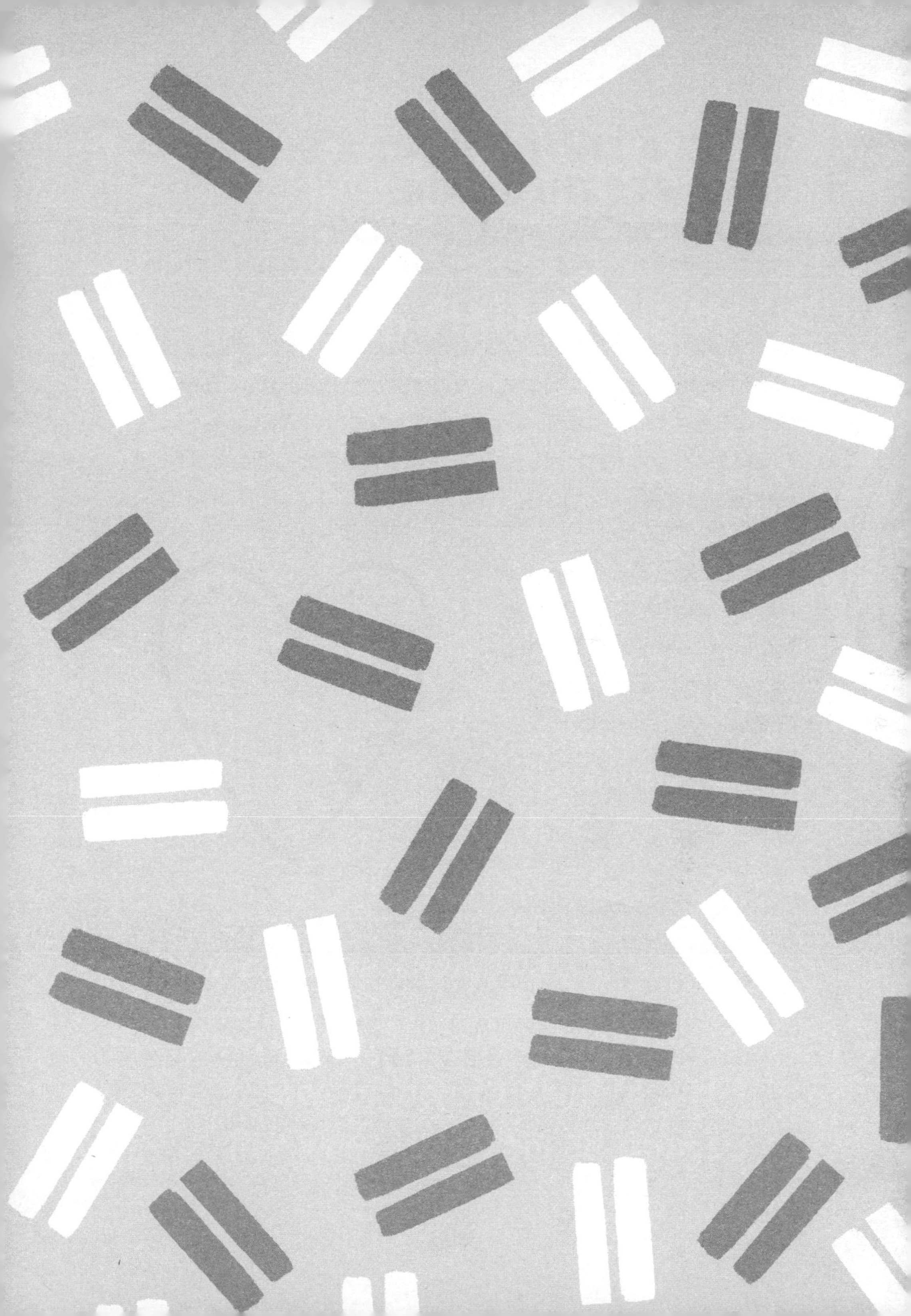

BEING A SHINY THING & SHOWING VAMPIRES THE DOOR,
SUSAN WOKOMA, ACTOR

Last night I was sat on the sofa in my friend Zak's living room in Manchester, nursing a red wine and discussing paint samples for his bedroom wall. This sounds like hellishly dull business but I assure you one day such genteel (aka boring) activities will be positively blissful.

You see, I met Zak when I was around 16 or 17. We have been through it all – youth theatre, first hangovers, first loves, coming outs, stayings in. Trust me when I say at 33 we have EARNED our boring nights in.

This is the longest time I have been single since I was 18 – a year and nine months at the time of writing this. It was a conscious decision, initially for a year, but Covid has dragged that kicking and screaming into two. And, like all my beautifully coupled-up friends, Zak is eager to see his Susie in love again (or at least on the pull). The thing is reader, I made a discovery in the last year that I wish I had been made aware of when I was your age. So here it goes:

I'm a shiny thing. Yup. I'm shiny. I'm glossy and shiny and funny and ATTRACTIVE. No – not in the Rihanna sense – but I bring value. And guess what readers? I had no idea!

None.

That's because I was told from a very young age (too young) that I wasn't worth much – by everything from advertising to magazine covers to movies to strangers to even some of those close to me. And I believed it. I really did. Shiny people were Britney Spears and S Club 7. Me, and people who looked like me, and came from where I came from, were ordinary. We were

Thing is, if you don't know your worth, someone will exploit whatever remains of it.

And that's what happened to me – in romance, at work, within friendship groups. People saw that innate shine and started stomping it out, or stealing it, or loving and praising it, only to then resent it. These people – let's call them 'vampires' – came real thick and fast, and I could not understand why I was attracting them.

So I'm here now sat [sitting?] with Zak and we are talking about what we wish we knew when we were teenagers. What are the things in our 30s that we are still trying to unpick? And let me tell you this reader, if you have true love and respect for yourself, if you can really sizzle in your own company, enjoy the quiet of your own magical breath, then any vampire that tries to steal your shine, will fail ...

We hear the terms 'self-love' and 'self-care' – the latter I have tattooed on my arm – but I'm not talking pampering face masks, airplane mode and Netflix. I mean real, deep, euphoric appreciation and admiration for yourself. This is not narcissism. It is gratitude, for everything you tried and failed at, for everything you succeeded at, for every hair on your head.

Fall in love with yourself. When you forget or falter (and my darling hun, you will), ask your friends why they love you. I really wish someone had told me how lovely I was, 'cos maybe when the vampires arrived, I would have very quickly told them: 'No, you can leave me alone, I'm good, thanks!' A dear friend of mine once said

if you don't know who you are, someone else will tell you

Another boring thing I love are morals. I'm not talking monks and stern headteachers barking stuff at you, I mean connecting to what is right and wrong and consequences and empathy. As I have got older, I feel like in order to be 'cool' I have had to invite (even create) chaos into my life and inflict it on others.

Chaos is something often revered in my career as an actor. Being deep and dangerous has long been associated with 'genius' or 'creativity'. There is an idea that art is created through pain but I've never subscribed to that – I had a project in my second year of drama school that was so horrific that I vowed to never, ever bring my trauma to work again! But outside of the Arts, 'grey areas' are being celebrated. And yes, putting binaries in the bin when it comes to gender and sexuality is WHAT WE WANT!

But how we treat people? How we love people? How we empathise? I don't see kindness and transparency as a thing up for debate. And yet at one point calling out abusive behaviour was seen as me just being bitter – why couldn't I just swallow it and internalise all that? Why was I making a big deal out of it? 'Yes, but they're a genius/Yes, but they're troubled and have been hurt and are very talented.'

I tried this shoe on for about a year and then burnt it. Morals matter. Right and wrong is clear. Absorbing abuse is what I decided to leave in 2019. I decided to break free and do things my way. I believe you can be the most 'dangerous', 'unpredictable' and 'exciting' artist and still treat people with kindness. You can still go wild and create stories for the memoirs whilst treating people with respect. Life is messy enough as it is without being destructive.

Live and move and work from love. I can't tell you how much I mean that. The opposite of fear is love. So have love for others, but most importantly,

fall madly in love with yourself.

And buy some garlic.

And maybe a crucifix.

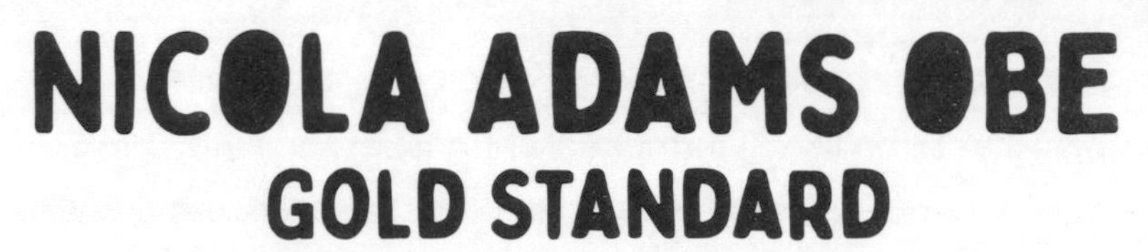

'The most important thing is to be honest about yourself. Secrets weigh heavy and it's when you try to keep everything to yourself that it becomes a burden. You waste energy agonising when you could be living your life and realising your dreams.'

As women, we've had to fight for our right to vote, to own property, not to be (quite literally) owned by a man – but it's hard to imagine that a sport and hobby enjoyed by many was banned for over fifty percent of the population. But until 1996, that was boxing.

But the year the ban was lifted, 13-year-old Nicola Adams took to the ring and began to change history! Inspired by a legendary fight between Muhammad Ali and George Foreman in 1974, Nicola decided she wanted to be just like Ali, and while she was the only girl at her gym, she didn't let that deter her.

She took part in an England boxing camp in 2001 and was called up to box for her country not long afterwards. She hasn't looked back since. But it wasn't until 2009 that Women's Boxing was officially recognised and added to the Olympic Programme at London 2012. There she won GB's first-ever female boxing gold and became a fighting icon. The 2016 Olympics in Rio de Janeiro brought further success when Nicola became a double Olympic champion winning her second gold medal.

There is no doubt Nicola Adams is a superhero of British sport, not only for her talent and work ethic, but also for her support of the LGBTQ+A community. She competed as half of the first-ever same-sex pair on the popular TV show, *Strictly Come Dancing,* and is known for her powerful messages of confidence, empowerment and self-belief, encouraging girls and women that they can do absolutely anything they put their minds to.

So, be more Nicola Adams, roll with life's punches, and never be afraid to fight back (metaphorically of course!). And finally, repeat after me ladies:

Say it three times in your mirror every morning, then go out into the world and achieve your dreams!

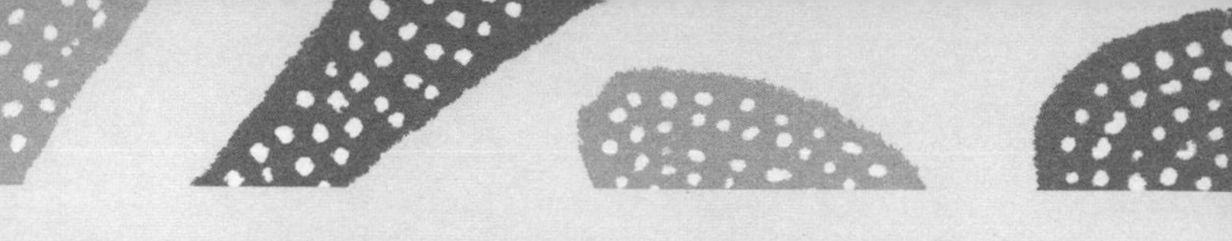

FIND YOUR HAPPY, EMILY COXHEAD, CREATOR OF 'THE HAPPY NEWS'

Dear Teenage Em,

Happiness is and always has been a huge part of your life, you've been very lucky to have been surrounded by love and happiness your entire life and I want you to know that, as clichéd as it sounds, it really is the most important thing. It's more important than any grade you will get, which I know is hard to see right now, but trust me that D in German is *not* worth losing sleep over... oh and spoiler alert; you pass your Maths GCSE! Woohoo! You will never do anything other than basic maths again and you can have a pretty incredible job being creative, so do keep quietly ignoring anyone who says otherwise. You'll prove them wrong.

I know that happiness is something you already consider in the decisions you make, but it will play a huge role in your life as you get older. You'll even win 'Biggest Grin Award' when you leave secondary school. Now, unfortunately you can't get a job with this qualification, but it might make sense when you set up your own

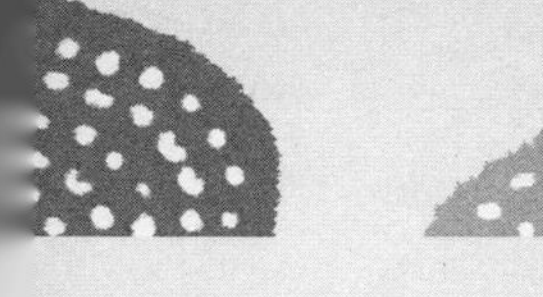

business. (Oh yeah, by the way, you set up your own business a few years from now! How cool is that?)

I could warn you about all the good and bad things that will happen, but you need to experience these to shape you into the person you will become. Things won't always be happy, but when things get really, really messy I just want you to know that they *will* get better. See, sometimes our very best moments can come from our very worst and, without giving too much away, you manage to turn the most difficult time of your life into a positive to help other people find some happy in their darkest moments too ... that's a pretty incredible thing.

There will be stuff I could tell you not to do and boys I could tell you to stay away from, but things work out pretty good in the end and I think you need to experience the whole thing to appreciate how it all turns out. You might be an overthinker most of the time, but you also

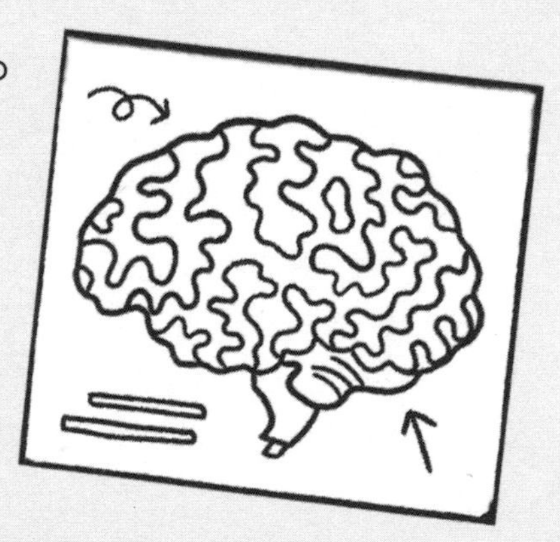

don't let anyone take the mick out of you, which means that when it comes to the big stuff you usually make the right choices. You won't always make the right decisions but that's how you

learn and grow!

Just know that your shattered trust and broken heart will be fixed, it takes a little while but (when you meet him) he will 'get you', you'll laugh at stupid stuff daily and be able to talk about the rubbish stuff when life gets too much. You will be the very best team; trust me on that and don't let him go.

There will always be people throughout your life who take away some of your sparkle and, I know your mum always tells you this, but it really does say far more about them than it does about you. You feel people's emotions and pain more than most people I know, and that can be a real weight to carry around at times, especially when you're struggling yourself. So please learn to try and share the load, talk to somebody you trust and know that you can't fix everything or everyone.

You will find 'your people', some of them are your best pals right now and some will come into your life when you need it most. These people are like sunshine and warm hugs and make you do that 'cackle' when you properly start laughing, or will sit with you and a cup of tea for hours. It's easier said than done but consider who you have around you and try to surround yourself with good people. You might be one on your own at times (most of the time – you still really need your own space by the way!) but you'll also have some very special people in your world.

Continue to focus on the stuff you're passionate about, keep drawing, writing and taking photos.

'Don't waste your talent',

as Miss Hamblett says in your school yearbook. I can't even begin to tell you about all the absolutely mental things you're going to do and achieve; you wouldn't believe me if I told you but keep working hard and whatever you do don't give up on those dreams! Oh, and on the work thing ... try not to work too much. Your work and passion will become your biggest focus and although amazing and wonderful, don't forget to rest, take care of you and have some fun! This all sounds incredibly boring but you understand you and your body more than I think you realise at times, so listen to it. I promise your life won't be boring, you go to Glastonbury ... and America! On your own!

Classic you, you've never had a plan or an idea of what your life is going to look like and right now as grown up Em, I'm not exactly sure what the future holds for you but what I do know is that you've made it your mission to focus on the good and share that with as many people as you can. I'm so sure that there will continue to be an abundance of happiness in your life as you get older, and also some sad and painful stuff too, but remember to keep that happy jar topped up as often as you can.

Know that grief and sadness often come from the immense amount of love and happy memories we have with those around us. Your joy will continue to be passed on to those around you and there's already two little humans (your nieces) who share that joy; they remind you how much you loved crafting, making dens and baking when you were little (and still do). Being an Auntie is the best!

Trust that things might not always go as expected, but you always seem to have had a way of carving your own way in this world and if the last few years has taught you anything it's that you can cope with far more than you give yourself credit for. You've never loved change and can often feel overwhelmed, but you always seem to figure it out.

I don't tell you enough, but you should be so proud of yourself.

Lots of love from Em x

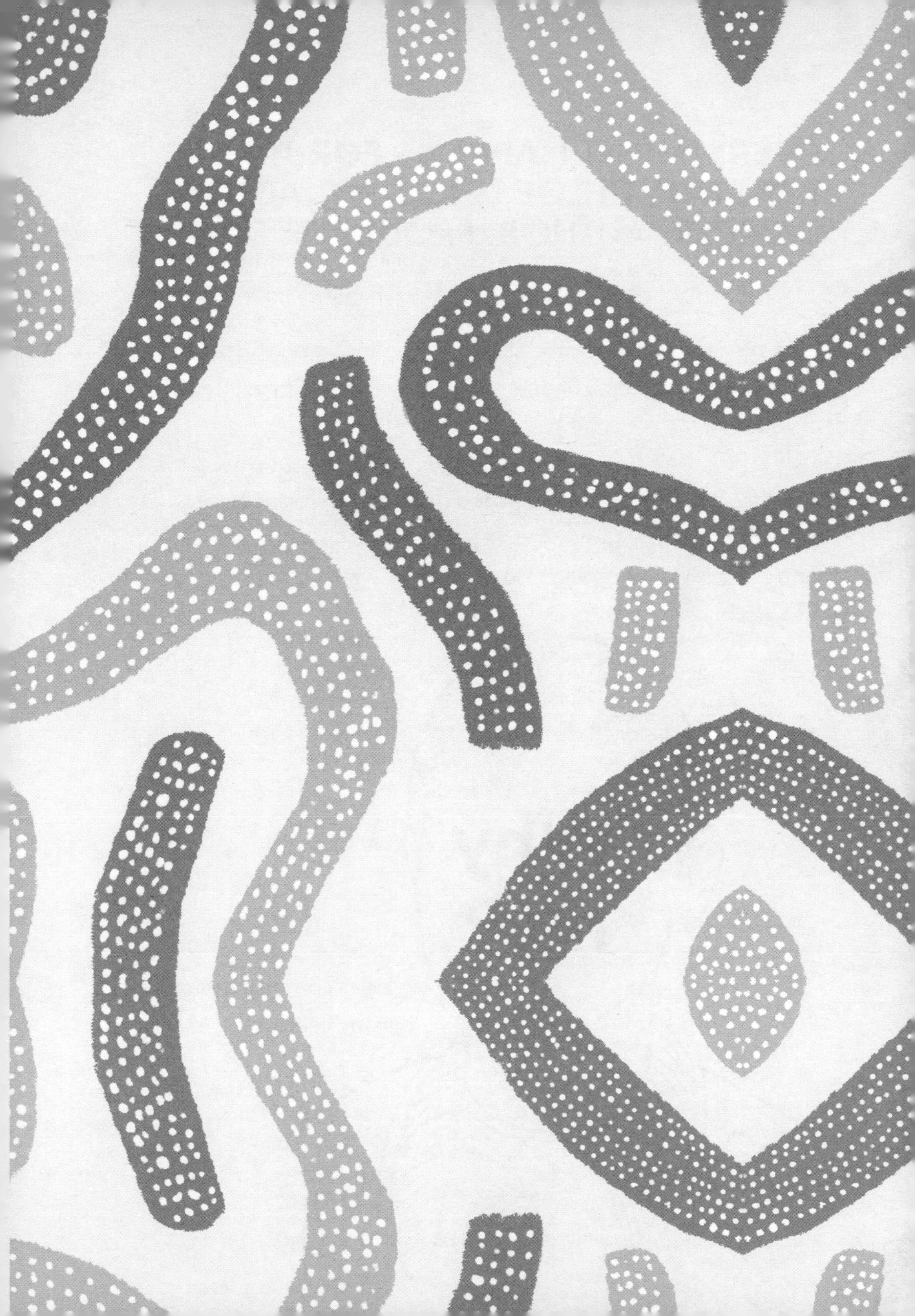

EVERYTHING HAPPENS FOR A REASON', CHLOE LUKASIAK, ACTOR, DANCER, AUTHOR, PRODUCER

I live, breathe, and die by the above quote. And when you realise the truth of 'everything happens for a reason', a weight is lifted off of you.

But it took me a while to accept and understand this idea, and until I did, I was constantly frustrated at the world, with my life, with the things I was going through.

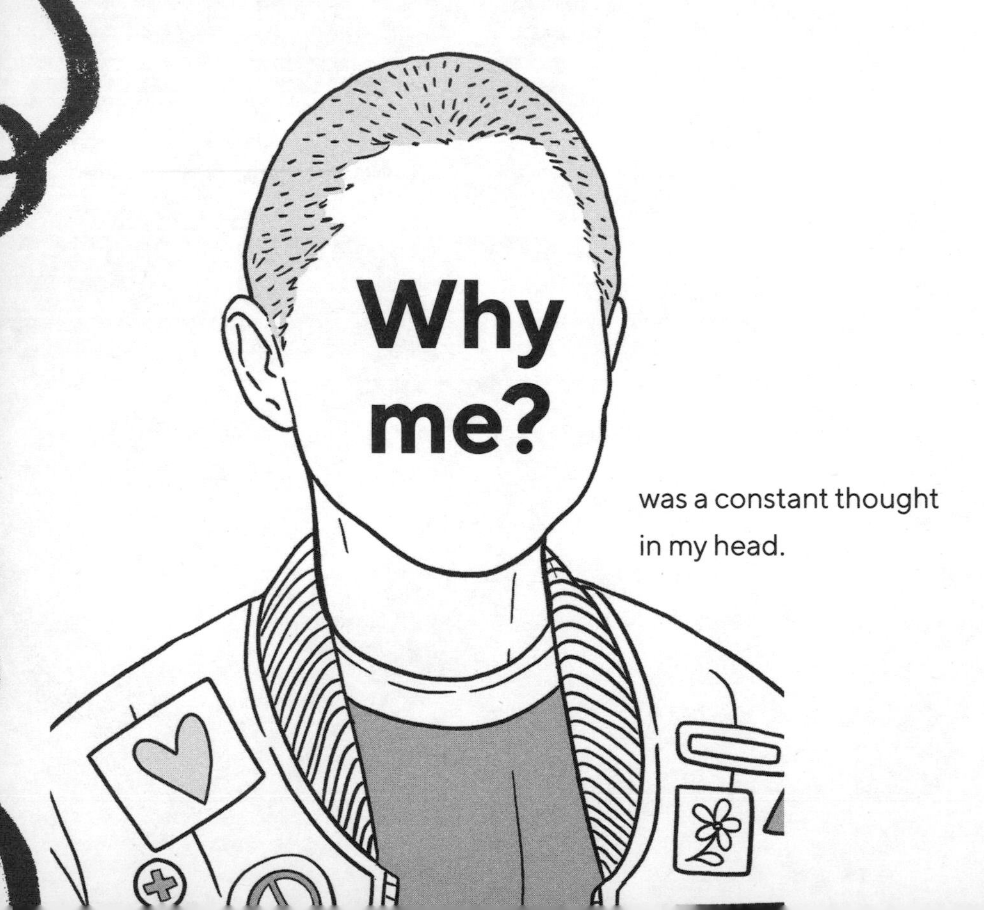

Why me?

was a constant thought in my head.

I would find myself getting defeated by the smallest setbacks and instead of being inspired by unexpected things, I was always floored by them. I had a negative outlook on a lot of things and I didn't see the purpose in everything I was going through. Rejections from roles I really wanted and also online bullying was having a really bad effect on me. It wasn't until I was about 18 years old that I really began to start considering all that had happened to me, the path I was on, and where I was going.

It was then that I decided to change the narrative in my head and instead of thinking 'Why me?' I started to think

'Yay me!'.

But let's wind back a bit ...

When I was 8 years old, I was leading a very ordinary life in Pittsburgh, Pennsylvania. I went to school, I did competitive dance in the afternoons, and spent my weekends playing baseball with my dad in the street. I figured I would probably pursue dance professionally when I got older, but didn't think about my adult years too much. Everything was simple. And then a year later, I was on a reality television show. Certainly not a twist I expected. I experienced difficult times during the 4 years I was on it and then for the following years after. I left the show and decided I wanted to continue being part of the entertainment industry. I continued dancing and ended up touring the world, performing for more people than I could imagine and seeing places I never thought I'd see.

Then I started auditioning for TV shows and movies, and a few years later, I wound up in Vancouver, Canada, filming my first movie *Center Stage: On Pointe*. Soon after that, I decided I wanted to write an autobiography. I have loved books since I was a little girl. They have always been a very large part of my life. Never did I expect to write my very own. And here I am, writing (a small part of) a book again.

I gave you that very brief overview of my life for a reason. Not because I wanted to tell you about the book I wrote or the movies I filmed, but rather that I never expected my life to go the way it has. Little 8-year-old me playing baseball in the street never expected that 11 years later, I would be living in Los Angeles living the life I live.

People often ask me if I could travel back in time, what would I change? And my answer is the same every time: nothing.

I would change nothing in my life.
I always say I am grateful for everything
I have gone through.

When I say that, I don't necessarily mean I feel gratitude for the things I've gone through, but rather grateful that my journey has led me to the life I live now. Knowing that

has helped me live my life so fully. I don't feel defeat or frustration anymore. Because once you've gone through any sort of suffering or obstacle it gives you a perspective on things and gratitude towards everything. Instead of living in a mindset of negativity and victimhood, I choose to believe that I went through the things I did so that it would make me the person I have become, and taught me the lessons I needed to learn.

When I experience something difficult like being rejected from a role or dealing with insincere people, I remind myself that it is happening for a reason, whether it be to teach me a lesson or take me somewhere new in life. I know that there is a purpose for everything I experience; that you will get through whatever you are going through and will be better for it. Understanding this idea also changes your perspective on regrets. There is no point in having regrets or looking back at situations and wishing you could change them. They happened exactly as they were supposed to. There is so much peace that comes with this mindset shift. I hope you find peace knowing that everything that has happened to

you and will happen to you is for a reason. I hope you find your own peace and learn to see the purpose for everything.

PLAY THE LEAD IN YOUR OWN LIFE – DON'T BE A BIT PART, CARRIE HOPE-FLETCHER, ACTOR & WRITER

A question I ask myself a lot is:

'What do I want my life to look like when I reminisce at the ripe old age of 90?'

I've always been a classic overthinker and have been known to plan for years in advance when I have no idea what I'm even cooking for dinner that very night. So, this question has always intrigued me ...

My answer has stayed relatively the same throughout the years. I want the story of my life to look colourful, bold and vibrant. And I want there to be a plethora of days that jump out as really great ones. Not days that I merely existed through, but days I really lived. I want to have loved as hard as I can, and feel so loved in return that the thought of it makes me weep.

I dread the idea that a year's worth of days will start to blend into one and begin to look grey and monotonous. Nothing scares me more than a half-lived and boring life. But it took me a long time to realise that a life like the one I wanted to live wouldn't just happen. As much as I love the idea of fate, destiny, paths that have been mapped out for us and stars aligning, I still feel like we must be actively seeking to ignite a chain reaction of *fortunate* events to occur. I have always believed

We need to be the catalyst. We have to fan our own flames.

I really only began to understand this when I played the part of Eponine in London's West End musical *Les Misérables* when I was 20. As much as I *love* Eponine, and had wanted to play her since

I was seven years old, I had to admit that not only is she not the main character in *Les Misérables*, she's also not even the main character in her own story. In my opinion – though some may passionately disagree – Eponine is merely a side character in Marius' story … and *Les Misérables* isn't even about Marius! He's a side character in Valjean's story. By this logic, Eponine is the side character in a side character's story! Everything she does is for someone else. She even dies for the man she loves who has barely even looked at her twice …

Through this, I started to realise that I was also playing a bit part in my own life.

Everything I did centred around something or someone else. My parents, someone I was dating, my work or my friends. I said 'yes' to everything and then figured out how to do it all later, because disappointing someone was a no-go. I couldn't bear letting anyone down. I couldn't bear ruining a chapter in someone else's story because I wasn't pulling my weight. Never did I stop and say

'Hang on a minute. What is my story?
How can I tell it better?

How can I become the leading lady of
my own life instead of doing everything
I can to facilitate everyone else's?'

I realised I needed to figure out what my goal was and what I needed to do in order to achieve that. It took me far too long to learn that it's okay to say no sometimes in order to focus on what will make *you* happy or what will help you tell your story better. If you're a people-pleaser like me, it feels extraordinarily selfish, but sometimes, that's okay. Sometimes, that's necessary. Sometimes you just need to figure out what you're doing before you can even think about helping someone else.

Another barrier that kept me from being my own leading lady, long before I was even in a musical, was convincing myself via social media that everyone else had a much better story to tell.

My story felt phenomenally BORING compared to the lives portrayed online. Everyone else seemed so 'put together', so glossy and perfect. I'd lust over photos of tanned goddesses prancing on golden beaches while I sweat through my jumper running for the tube. I'd drool over pics of perfectly cooked steak and the thinnest cut French fries from restaurants my bank account wouldn't allow me to visit, while I ate cheese on toast

for the fourth night in a row. Someone was always writing their second book of the year or reading their fiftieth; someone had run one hundred miles in a month raising thousands for charity or someone had just landed my dream role or had just got engaged and the rock in their ring was bigger than my face. And everyone looked fitter and healthier and happier and I...

Well ...

... I was sat in four-week-old pyjamas on my mum and dad's sofa eating a family sized bag of

Doritos in front of rubbish daytime telly. Is that a story anyone wants to tell or even hear for that matter? I didn't think so.

Despite the fact I learnt the vital lesson that what people portray online isn't real life, it's a highlight reel, I also got infinitely bored of the sound of life whizzing by me. Of opportunities whooshing past that I didn't grasp because I was scared or already so bogged down by a million favours I'd said yes to because I didn't know how to say *no*.

So, I decided something needed to change. I wanted to be one of those people living the life they'd always dreamed of. I wanted to write a book and eat posh steak in fancy restaurants. I wanted to run long distances and raise money for charities. I wanted to play a leading lady on a West End stage as well as be my *own* main character. But none of that would happen if I didn't take the steps to do it. You've gotta be in it to win it. You won't win the lottery if you don't buy a ticket. If you don't stand up and say

THIS IS *MY* STORY

and stop acting like a sidekick, you'll never be the lead in your own life story! And EVERYONE deserves to be the lead of their own life. Your story is worth telling. Even if you don't think so right now.

When you're 90 years old and someone asks you what your life was like, you're not going to want to shrug and say it was 'just okay', that there were no memorable moments, that you never did *anything* interesting. You'll want to say you were happy and lived the life you'd always wanted to, no matter shape that might take.

We all have different definitions of success and happiness, and we all have different aspirations and ambitions. So whatever your story is, tell it with your chest puffed out and proud, your chin up and your voice strong and clear.

So don't be a bit part, play the lead in your own story – and the rest will follow!

10 THINGS YOU CAN DO TO TAKE UP SPACE IN THE WORLD

1 SORRY, NOT SORRY

There are clear and obvious times when an apology is needed, but women often find themselves apologising for simply existing and, frankly, it's a habit we need to get out of. How many times do you find yourself saying sorry in a day? For silly things, like simply walking into a room, misunderstanding something or even (classic) when someone bumps into YOU! We have to stop this. Practice alternative ways of saying 'sorry' like 'Unfortunately, I didn't hear you, could you repeat that' Or if really you do need to say sorry, say it once and move on.

USE YOUR VOICE 2

Women often speak faster because we're used to getting cut off, interrupted or not being heard. So slow down when you speak and use your voice proudly, it's the strongest thing you have. Use your voice to advocate for yourself, for others or for a cause – and throw your weight behind things you really care about.

3 STAND TALL

Don't feel the need to make yourself smaller, to not take up much room or space, or be a nuisance. Instead, **stand tall** with your **shoulders back, your head held high**, **your chin up**, and **make room for yourself**. Know and believe that you have just as much right to be in the room as anyone else.

4 LOOK INTO MY EYES!

So often when we feel shy, awkward or uncomfortable, we find ourselves looking anywhere but at the person we're talking to. But an important way for young women to convey confidence and self-esteem is through maintaining eye contact. It also shows that you are listening and engaged in the conversation and that you are confident about what you're saying.

5 BE DIRECT

If you want to come across self-assured and confident in what you are saying (and who doesn't?), then try to avoid using tag questions like 'Don't you think?' at the end of sentences, or weak phrases like 'I'm not sure/I'm not an expert in this but ...' Both of these can convey that you are less confident and competent than you really are. I don't know about you, but I very rarely hear men using these sorts of phrases! Be clear, confident and forthright in what you're saying – and that includes less humming and hawing, too ...

6 THE POWER POSE

This is a BRILLIANT 'trick' to play on your mind when you need a bit of a confidence boost, such as when walking into a party, before an exam or interview, or any time you feel a bit nervous. So, you stand in a posture that you mentally associate with being powerful (think Super Girl with your arms and legs in a strong, starfish-type pose!). This is called Power Posing, and will make you feel more powerful and confident. Stand in this pose for a minute or two while taking a few deep breaths (you can do it in a loo cubicle so that people don't give you funny looks!) Trust me, it will make you feel like taking up space!

7 PRODUCTIVITY DOES NOT EQUAL WORTH

Always remember your self-worth and how much you achieve in a day, month or year has nothing to do with what a valuable human being you are. Sure, productive days are great, but days where you rest and make time for self-care are just as important, and will help you take up space in the world when you are ready!

8 TRUST YOUR GUT

To be able to take up space in the world, you need to trust in your gut. Your instinctive feelings are valid so never let anyone tell you don't or that you are not allowed to feel a certain way. Hold on tight to how you feel; people may try to manipulate your emotions or even 'gaslight' you, but never ignore your gut instinct, as it won't lead you far wrong.

9 BE PASSIONATE

Passion and enthusiasm are infectious! And passionate people draw others to them. It's better to be someone who LOVES things, than someone who acts as if they're over everything. (Because they're not, they're totally pretending not to care!) So if you're a Number 1 Fan of something or someone, or if you love a particular hobby or even TV show – share your passion. You'll inspire people and take up your space in the world by being yourself, and being infectiously enthusiastic.

THERE'S NO SUCH THING AS COOL 10

Being cool. Being 'it'. Being 'on trend'. None of it matters, except what YOU think is cool. Trends change *all* the time (I did the 90's thing the first time around – I thought it was cool!) so don't worry about what everyone else is doing. Take up your own space.

YOU
DO
YOU
PEARLY WHITES
Shine Crème
MASCARA

RESOURCES TO SEEK FURTHER SUPPORT ON SOME OF THE ISSUES RAISED IN THIS BOOK

stem4.com

A leading teenage mental health charity, where you can find advice, help and apps to aid your mental wellbeing.

teenagearmageddon.co.uk

Our kick-ass website! Find out more about Teenage Armageddon, the podcast, the play and with a blog covering a whole host of subjects, amazing guest writers, practical top tips and self care.

iamarla.com

A community to support young women and girls who have experienced abuse, trauma and discrimination.

bloodygoodperiod.com

An amazing charity who provides period products to those who can't afford them, and menstrual education to those less likely to access it. And they help everybody talk about periods!

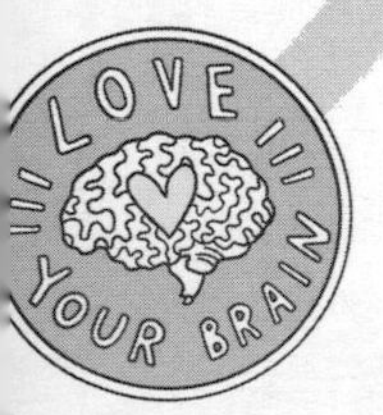

everyonesinvited.uk

Everyone's Invited is a movement and an organisation focused on exposing and tackling rape culture through conversation, education and support.

womensmediacenter.com/fbomb

An intersectional teen feminist media platform created by and for socially conscious youth.

stonewall.org.uk

Stonewall campaigns for the equality of lesbian, gay, bi and trans people across the UK.

thetrevorproject.org

The Trevor Project is the leading national organisation providing crisis intervention and suicide prevention services to lesbian, gay, bisexual, transgender, queer & questioning youth.

mermaidsuk.org.uk

A charity supporting gender diverse young people.

girlup.org

A movement to advance girls' skills, rights, and opportunities to be leaders.

amightygirl.com

The world's largest collection of books, activities and movies for smart, confident, and courageous girls.

whenateengoesgreen.com

An amazing blog centred around eco-positive living, and how we can adapt our lifestyle to help the planet.

healthforteens.co.uk

Health for Teens offers a great choice of content, advice and answers to your questions across all areas of your health.

youthaccess.org.uk

Youth Access is an advice and counselling network for teens, a place for you to talk through any problems.

everdayfeminism.com

Everyday Feminism is an educational platform for personal and social liberation of women.

REFERENCES

Dolly Parton

https://dollyparton.com

Nicola Adams

https://nicola-adams.com

Katie Piper

https://katiepiperfoundations.org.uk

Emma Gonzalez

https://variety.com/2018/politics/features/emma-gonzalez-parkland-interview-1202972485

Alexandra Ocasio-Cortez

https://ocasio-cortezhouse.gov
https://time.com
https://www.vanityfair.com/news/2020/10/becoming-aoc-cover-story-2020

https://**www.eif.org.uk**/report/adolescent-mental-health-evidence-brief-1-prevalence-of-disorders

https://www.google.co.uk/amp/s/amp.theguardian.com/society/2019/jun/04/one-in-five-young-women-have-self-harmed-study-reveals

https://www.google.co.uk/amp/s/amp.theguardian.com/society/2018/aug/29/quarter-of-14-year-old-girls-in-uk-have-self-harmed-report-finds

https://**youngminds.org.uk**/about-us/reports/coronavirus-impact-on-young-people-with-mental-health-needs/#covid-19-summer-2020-survey

https://**www.mentalhealth.org.uk**/news/teenagers-mental-health-pandemic

ACKNOWLEDGEMENTS

Instructions for a Teenage Armageddon was a tiny idea I had one day, inspired by the incredible work of the stem4 team and our fearless leader Dr Nihara Krause, without whom this book would not exist.

And I guess without my parents, I would not exist! Mum and dad, I got pretty lucky to have parents as supportive as you. My mum is one of the original kick-ass women, and I wouldn't be who I am without you both. The same goes for my sister Sophie, had she not entered into the entertainment world first, I would never have found it myself, so I guess Soph, you are the reason for all of this. Thank you. (And to my brother Michael, who everyone forgets exists, thank you for supporting my feminism when I was 15, and buying me all the books.)

To Hannah Price and Georgie Straight who helped create *Teenage Armageddon*, I am so incredibly lucky to get to not only work with you both, but call you both friends. You are two of the most luminous, brilliant women I know.

Anna Dixon, super-agent extraordinaire, who took an idea, turned into a reality, and held my hand every step of the way – thank you. Your constant ideas, help and utter belief in this project and me has meant the world. And Alex Bewley and the whole WME team – I am so grateful to have your support and to get to work with you.

To our incredible editor Debbie Foy, whose guidance and faith in this project has been truly invaluable – thank you for all your hard work and for being so kind throughout! And to Ruth Alltimes, and the entire team at Wren & Rook – what a total honour to have my first book published by you. I still can't believe it!

To our amazing contributors, who believed in this enough to come on board, there are not enough thanks I can give for lending your time and thoughts. And Nadia Akingbule – thank you for bringing this book alive with your amazing illustrations. Your talent blows me away.

To Kevin Proctor, who really is the person behind all this being possible – but I know he will take no credit. My only wish is that everyone could have a producer as stunning as you, no one works harder to see a dream through.

Brian Zeilinger-Goode, Perry Trevers, Nicola Pearcey and everyone at Studio POW, I don't know what I did to get to work with such kind, incredible people, but I feel like I've won the lottery. To Phil and Beth, for your unwavering support (and constantly feeding me) and to Millie and Charlotte – the two most brilliant teenage girls upon whom all of this is based.

Charlie (Cha cha), Fraser, Lucy, Shene, Millie, Jess – you know what I think of you all, thank you for standing by me through out everything. Molly, Matilda, Tiggy, Teddy and Phantom – yes, I'm thanking my cats here – but who else sat with me while I worked on this and distracted me with their cuteness?

And lastly the women who kept me going throughout my own teenage years: Caitlin Moran and Taylor Swift. The real MVPs.

Rosie Day

New Approaches to
Welfare Theory

1852789816